"On Rising Ground"

John M. Douthit, March 1862.

Courtesy of Elaine Palencia

"On Rising Ground"

The Life and Civil War Letters of
John M. Douthit,
52nd Georgia Volunteer Infantry Regiment,
C.S.A.

ELAINE FOWLER PALENCIA

MERCER UNIVERSITY PRESS
Macon, Georgia

MUP/ H997

© 2021 by Mercer University Press
Published by Mercer University Press
1501 Mercer University Drive
Macon, Georgia 31207
All rights reserved

25 24 23 22 21   5 4 3 2 1

Books published by Mercer University Press are printed on acid-free
paper that meets the requirements of the American National Standard
for Information Sciences—Permanence of Paper for Printed Library
Materials.

Printed and bound in the United States.

This book is set in Adobe Caslon Pro.

Cover/jacket design by Burt&Burt.

ISBN   978-0-88146-766-6

Library of Congress Control Number: 2020948136

Cataloging-in-Publication Data is available from the Library of Congress

For the Descendants of John Douthit, Sr.

(b. Ireland, 1709–d. North Carolina, 1784),

Great-great-grandfather of John M. Douthit (1837–1863)

MERCER UNIVERSITY PRESS

Endowed by

TOM WATSON BROWN
and
THE WATSON-BROWN FOUNDATION, INC.

Contents

List of Illustrations and Photographs

Preface

For decades the fading photocopies were passed from family member to family member, until no one remembered where some of the originals were to be found. There were thirty-one letters in all: twenty-eight letters written by John M. Douthit to his wife, Martha Willson Douthit, and two letters from John to his sister-in-law, Julietta Condecy Willson, all written during John's Civil War service; and one letter from a neighbor and fellow soldier, Benjamin F. Tilley, to Martha. John's letters were written from March 1862 to May 1863 during his time with the 52nd Georgia Volunteer Infantry Regiment, Company H. This regiment was part of the brigade formed by north Georgia men at Camp McDonald in early 1862 and that, in its final form, also included the 40th, 41st, 42nd, and 43rd regiments. It has come to be known as the Barton-Stovall Brigade for its two commanders, Seth Maxwell Barton[1] and Marcellus Augustus Stovall.[2]

The letters went by post or were hand-carried from campsites and hospitals in Georgia, Tennessee, Kentucky, and Mississippi to Martha back in Fannin County, Georgia, where John had been a farmer before the start of the Civil War. One original letter was passed down through the Cochran family, into which John's and Martha's daughter Victoria married, and

---

[1] Barton (1829–1900) was a native of Virginia and a graduate of West Point. He would be with this brigade until the fall of Vicksburg. Subsequently he commanded a different brigade in Virginia. After the war he became a noted chemist.

[2] Stovall (1819–1895), of Sparta, Georgia, began his military career with the Georgia state militia, fought in the Seminole Wars, and served under several commanders before assuming leadership of the regiments that had fought with Barton.

finally to my mother, Rubye Cochran Fowler. Another original resides in the State of Georgia pension files. Martha had to give it up after the Civil War in order to receive a war widow's pension. The locations of the other originals are unknown to me. During the years of my research, I found another pertinent item in the National Archives: a letter from Martha's brother John Vandiver Willson to the United States Adjutant General, written in 1864 to inquire about John and his younger brother, Warren Davis Douthit, who also served in the Georgia 52nd.

John's epistolary style is indicative of his time and educational attainment. He clings to formulaic phrases, especially of greeting and farewell. Often he begins a letter with some variation of "I now take my pen in hand to write you a few lines to let you know that I am well," and just as often he closes, "Your husband until Death." In studying the personal correspondence of a Cornish family, the Clifts, who were writing letters in the 1790s, Francis Austin found set phrases similar to those we read in John's letters and in those by other lightly educated Civil War soldiers. She writes, "The formulaic phrasing that all the Clifts resort to, especially in the openings and endings of their letters, has its origins in letter writing manuals that can be traced back to the fourteenth and fifteenth centuries. Some go back even earlier to Anglo-Norman formularies of the tenth and eleventh centuries. By the second decade of the eighteenth century formulas had largely disappeared from the letters of literate and literary persons."[3] But they persisted longer among the working classes and certainly in north Georgia. John's dogged use of stock phrases may indicate that he viewed letters almost as official documents, like a court record, too rare and important for popular language. The set phrases tend to interfere with our

---

[3] Francis Austin, "Letter Writing in a Cornish Community in the 1790s," in David Barton and Nigel Hall, eds., *Letter Writing as a Social Practice* (Philadelphia: Jon Benjamins Publishing, 2000), 52–53.

view of events, and they took up space when paper was scarce. Still, his letters, tradition-bound as they are, shine a small but significant light on historical events.

The writer Ambrose Bierce, who served with the 9th Indiana Volunteer Infantry Regiment, wrote of individual fates during wartime, "There is a class of events which by their very nature, and despite any intrinsic interest that they may possess, are foredoomed to oblivion. They are merged in the general story of those greater events of which they were a part, as the thunder of a billow breaking on a distant beach is unnoted in the continuous roar."[4] Not only do John's letters fall into that category, but so does his life and the lives of so many unheralded soldiers like him. They are tiny waves in a vast ocean. Not even John's middle name has survived beyond the initial "M." The likeliest guess is that M stands for McClure, his mother's maiden name. Before the photocopies themselves fade, John's modest voice deserves to be preserved and to be heard again.

John M. Douthit was no Sam R. Watkins, the Tennessee soldier who authored *Co. Aytch*, one of the best accounts by an enlisted man to come out of the Civil War. "You see I remember the little things," Watkins pointed out.[5] John did not possess Watkins's powers of description or his passion for military service. But neither did he have the opportunity to recollect events in tranquility twenty years after the war, as Watkins did. For John never came home. Moreover, in his letters, John was uncomplaining and reticent to a fault, passing over many horrific events he witnessed without comment. Yet we know he was there—at Cumberland Gap and various sites in eastern Tennessee; in the Confederate invasion and retreat from

---

[4] Ambrose Bierce, *Ambrose Bierce's Civil War*, ed. William McCann (New York: Wings Books, 1996), 38.

[5] Sam R. Watkins, *Co. Aytch: A Confederate Memoir of the Civil War* (1882; repr., New York: Simon & Schuster, 2003), 168.

Kentucky; in middle Tennessee, at Chickasaw Bayou, Warrenton, and other places in the Vicksburg campaign. His letters, by their very understatement and brevity, may point to the inadequacy of words to convey the full force of his war experience. This does not mean he fails to convey the feeling of that experience. The letters bear sober witness to the plight of poor men caught up in a rich man's war.

The letters of this private, who in time was promoted to second sergeant, also show how little the common soldier understood of the big picture, living on rumors of fights to come and of possible furloughs, and on garbled news of outcomes. Bierce noted,

> It is seldom, indeed, that a subordinate officer knows anything about the disposition of the enemy's forces—except that it is unamiable—or precisely whom he is fighting. As to the rank and file, they can know nothing more of the matter than the arms they carry. They hardly know what troops are upon their own right or left the length of a regiment away. If it is a cloudy day they are ignorant even of the points of the compass. It may be said, generally, that a soldier's knowledge of what is going on about him is coterminous with his official relation to it and his personal connection with it; what is going on in front of him he does not know at all until he learns it afterward.[6]

I have tried to set these family letters in a historical and documentary context that will explain the where and what of John's service. It is not my purpose to retell the story of the Civil War. But I do sketch out the situations, military and social, that John and his regiment participated in, filling in gaps before, between, and after the run of letters. John, the 52nd, and Barton's Brigade are the threads I trace through the pattern of the war for the time of his service. For example, chapter 10,

---

[6] Bierce, *Ambrose Bierce's Civil War*, 39.

[Stevenson's Division at] "Champion Hill," gives a brief idea of the action only of General Carter L. Stevenson's division and, within that, primarily details pertaining to Barton's Brigade and the 52nd Georgia. Readers interested in a full treatment of the battle as well as the lead-up and aftermath, hour by hour, may turn to Timothy B. Smith's masterful *Champion Hill: Decisive Battle for Vicksburg.* We have no letter from John concerning Champion Hill, but it is part of our narrative. When possible, for corroboration and expansion of his letters, I use letters from other men of lower rank, who were not part of the decision-making and thus had a similarly limited perspective, both north Georgia soldiers in his brigade and Union counterparts.

John's story is also the story of the family he left behind. Therefore, I have also included chapters set on the home front before and after John's service. These sketch the society from which he went to war and, later, what happened to John's wife Martha and to her immediate family and neighbors during and after the conflict. Here a family connection to a bloody instance of Civil War vigilante justice in north Georgia, involving both family and onetime members of the Georgia 52nd, is highlighted. The consequences of a man going off to war and never returning home has reverberated through generations.

John M. Douthit's phrenological chart, front and back.

Courtesy of Elaine Palencia

Self esteem 6
Approbativeness 3
Firmness 7
Veneration 7
Hope 5
Faith 5
Benevolence 7
Mirth 5
Causality 4
Tune 4
Time 3
Weight 6
Form 3
Size 3
Order 5
Color 4

Camp Near Rutledge
Tennesee Octo 28th 1862.

1st Page

Dear Wife

We are now at Rutledge at the south
foot of Clinch mountain 33 miles North west of Knox
ville at the Camps occupied by this Brigade last
summer. I propose to give you a short history of
our march into and out of Kentucky. First I am
in Bartons Brigade and in Stevensons division
which consists of Bartons, Rains, and Taylors Brigades
On the night of the 17th Sept the Federals burnt
and blew up the most of their valuable property in
the Gap and when we was roused up at 3 o'clock A.M
the 18th we had many guesses at the meaning of the
fires and explosions and stood under arms till
about ten A.M. when we moved for the Gap and reached
this strong fortress after a winding march of 5 miles
and were well satisfied to find no foe to recieve us
Here we lay till 11 o'clock A.M. the 20th when we marched
in pursuit of the retreating foe and marching through
volumes of dust with very little and very bad water
fourteen miles we slept at the Cumberland ford
Rissing with the first peep of day we told off
16 miles through dust with little water which
brought us to Goose Creek. Here we failed to cook
Rations although we lay till 11 oclock A.M. of

John M. Douthit's letter to his wife, October 8, 1862.

Courtesy of Elaine Palencia

Apples and Sugar Cane were plenty along the road
and they served to slake our thirst many times
when we could not have got water. Orders were
very strict against taking any kind of property; but
despite of Orders I have seen the last hill in a potato patch demolished and the last Sugar Cane taken
from a patch and nearly a half Regiment in an
orchard at a time. Orders were very strict
against straggling from the Regt. but many nights
out of 45 men in our Company not more than twelve
would stack arms when we would halt. Octo 1st
An early start and hard march passed us through
Lawrenceburg and we passed the night two miles
from town. 2nd We passed through Rough & Ready
and were informed by ~~Genrl Burton that he~~
expecting to meet the enemy to day; So we march
5 miles toward Louisville and finding no foe we
turned and came again to Rough & Ready and
marched within two miles of Frankfort the Capitol of the State. We were very pleasantly located
here and remained here till 4 O'clock P.M. of the
4th day Octo. During the 4th Our head men were
engaged in making a Governor for Kentucky;
but he did not warm his seat for we left that
evening at quick time. We went through town
burnt the Car bridge and the horse bridge and
marched on till 3 O'clock A.M. of the 5th across the Country
to Versailes 14 miles from Frankfort— Continued

Payroll form with enlistment bounty.

Courtesy of National Archives

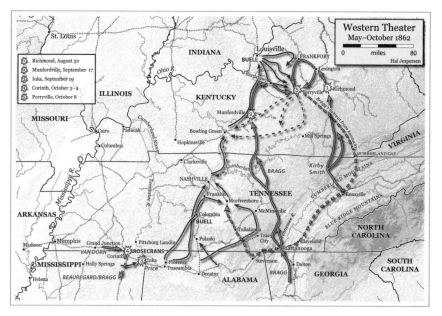

Western Theater, May to October 1862.

Courtesy of Hal Jesperson

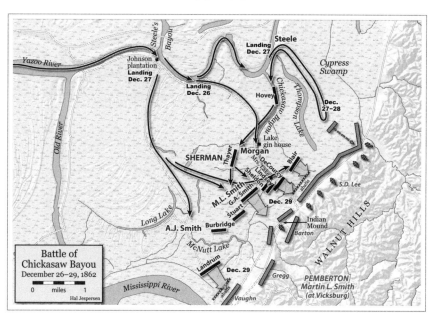

Battle of Chickasaw Bayou, December 26–29, 1862.

Courtesy of Hal Jesperson

Vicksburg Campaign
December 1862–April 1863

0   miles   50
Hal Jespersen

TENNESSEE
• Bolivar
• Memphis   Grand
             Junction
                                    Corinth •

ARKANSAS   Helena   GRANT ①
                      ② • Holly Springs • Ripley
      Coldwater R.

• St. Charles   • Oxford   • Tupelo
          ⑦   • Panola
McCLERNAND
                    Tallahatchie R.
Arkansas
• Post
Arkansas River
              Mississippi River
                                  Yalobusha R.
MISSISSIPPI   • Grenada
   DELTA   ⑧ Fort Pemberton
           • Greenwood   Columbus •

• Greenville   MISSISSIPPI
            Big Sunflower R.
                              Yazoo R.
                                    • Macon

                    • Yazoo City
Lake
Providence ⑥
           ③   ⑨   Big Black R.   Pearl R.
                            • Canton
SHERMAN   Steele's Bayou
          ⑩   Chickasaw Bayou   • Meridian
Duckport   • Vicksburg
          ⑤   • Warrenton • Raymond
New Carthage •   • JACKSON
                           • Raymond
          • Grand Gulf
Bruinsburg • • Port Gibson

• Natchez

① Central Mississippi Advance: ⑦ Yazoo Pass Expedition:
    November 14–December 21   February 3–April 10
② Holly Springs: December 20   ⑧ Fort Pemberton:
③ Chickasaw Bayou: December 27–29   March 11–April 5
④ Arkansas Post (Fort Hindman):   ⑨ Steele's Bayou Expedition:
    January 9–11   March 14–27
⑤ Grant's Canal: January 24–March 27 ⑩ Duckport Canal:
⑥ Lake Providence Expedition: March 31–April 11
    February 3–March 29

Vicksburg Campaign, December 1862 to April 1863.

Courtesy of Hal Jespersen

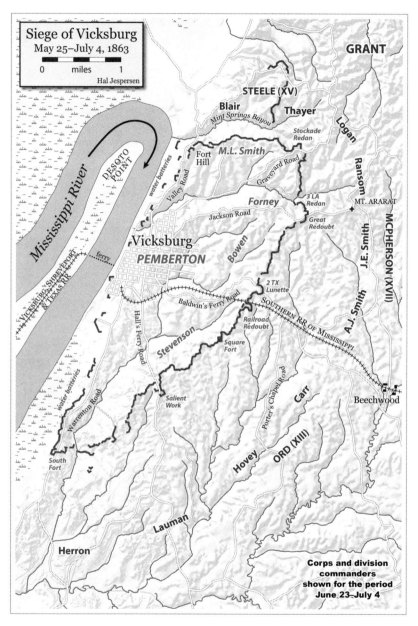

Siege of Vicksburg, May 25 to July 4, 1863.

Courtesy of Hal Jesperson

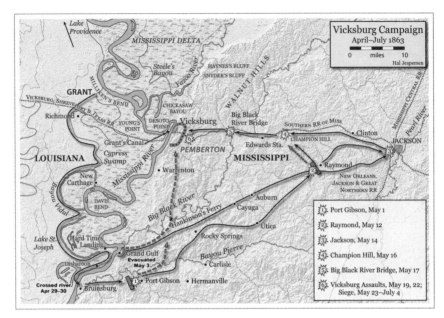

Vicksburg Campaign, April 1863 to July 1863.

Courtesy of Hal Jesperson

Washington Hotel and China Street, Vicksburg, Mississippi.

Courtesy of McArdle Library

Parole signed by John M. Douthit.

Courtesy of National Archives

Record of John M. Douthit's death and interment.

Courtesy of National Archives

Martha Willson Douthit Anderson.

Courtesy of Elaine Palencia

Martha Willson Douthit Anderson late in life.

Courtesy of Elaine Palencia

"On Rising Ground"

1

Birds in a Field

In July 1860, a census taker named Thomas Rhodes Trammell came to the north Georgia farming community of Hot House in Fannin County, just south of the Tennessee border, to enumerate its residents for the eighth US census.[1] Trammell, age thirty-two, a farmer who had served both as postmaster and sheriff, lived in the nearby district of Stock Hill and probably knew many of the families he called on. He would be counting free and enslaved residents, and fewer than thirty Cherokee.

Hot House was situated along Hot House Creek about six miles north of present-day Blue Ridge in what, only thirty years before, had been Cherokee country. The name *Hot House* referred to a Cherokee "sweat house," a low, log structure used in purification rituals. Plastered with clay to hold in heat, it contained a fire that was kept up in a special way. In cold weather, the elderly of the tribe were allowed to sleep in it.[2] Many other nearby place names lingered as reminders of the recently displaced indigenous population—the Toccoa River; Cohutta; Sugar Creek, whose name is derived from a

---

[1] Census information is taken from the US Federal Census Report of 1860 for Fannin County, GA.

[2] James Mooney, *Myths of the Cherokee and Sacred Formulas of the Cherokees* (Nashville, TN: Charles and Randy Elder Booksellers, 1982), 462.

vanished Cherokee Indian village called Kulse'tsi, meaning "sweet place" and referring to the honey locust,[3] and numerous others.

In 1820, the Cherokee population of north Georgia was estimated at 15,000.[4] The terrain—beautiful, mountainous, and crisscrossed with rivers and creeks—was less suited to raising cotton and to the establishment of plantations than the rest of the state and so at first did not draw great interest among white settlers. It was still largely wild. When author and explorer Charles Lanman visited the area in 1848, he noted, "This region is famous for the number and size of its rattlesnakes,"[5] and found the native Georgians to be "a very respectable class of people."[6] With the discovery of gold at Dahlonega in 1828, the coveting of Cherokee land commenced in earnest. The last land lotteries in Georgia, in 1832 and 1833, divided the area into lots and gave it to white settlers. In June 1838, following the "voluntary" removal of the Cherokee in 1836, the forced removal began via what came to be known as the Trail of Tears. The 1860 census of Fannin County shows that gold, as well as copper mines in the Copper Basin that reached into Tennessee, attracted mine workers from as far away as Germany and Cornwall, but farming remained the principal occupation.

On July 22, 1860, at household number 633 of the 908 households to be surveyed in the county, Trammell recorded details of a young married couple, John M. Douthit, age twen-

---

[3] Ken K. Krakow, *Georgia Place-Names*, 3rd ed. (Macon, GA: Winship Press, 1999), 214, online at http://www.kenkrakow.com/gpn/ georgia_place-names.htm.

[4] James C. Bonner, *A History of Georgia Agriculture 1732–1860* (Athens, GA: University of Georgia Press, 2009), 44.

[5] Charles Lanman, *Letters from the Alleghany Mountains* (New York: George P. Putnam, 1849), 13.

[6] Lanman, *Letters*, 16.

ty-three, and his wife Martha, twenty-two. John and Martha had married in August 1858, some four years after Fannin County was created out of Union and Gilmer counties. Though it was outside the purview of the census, we know that three weeks prior to the wedding, one Professor J. Denson did a phrenological reading of John, in which his score for "amativeness" was triple his score for "combativeness," with both outranked by the score for "sublimity."[7] Neither was there a place on the census form to note that Martha was expecting their first child, although presciently, the line below their names was left blank. Julietta Douthit, named for Martha's sister, would be born just over a month later, on August 26. John reported himself to be a farm hand with a personal estate valued at $200, a figure that would have included the worth of Martha's possessions as well. He did not own the land he farmed. But on the next farm, number 632, lived his widowed mother, Lilly Ann McClure Douthit, forty-nine, and four of his siblings, ranging in age from twenty-eight to twelve. John's father, a gunsmith also named John, had died in 1851. Lilly Ann Douthit listed land worth $3,000 and personal property valued at $500. Probably she owned the homestead of John and Martha. When her husband died, his estate included Cherokee land lots 157, 192–193, and 204–206 in the 8th district, second section.[8] John the gunsmith (1798–1851) and Lilly were both from South Carolina. Before coming to then Gilmer County, Georgia, they lived in McMinn County, Tennessee, where their son Solomon was born in 1830 and where their household included two enslaved people. By the time their son Robert was born in 1833, they

---

[7] "The Phrenological character of John M. Douthit as inferred by Prof. J. Denson July 24th 1858," photocopy of handwritten document. Owned by author. Phrenology, a pseudoscience popular in the nineteenth century, held that the conformation of the skull could be studied to discover qualities of character and personality.

[8] Fannin County, GA, Deed Book D, 308.

were living in northern Georgia. In 1836, John the gunsmith was deeded land in Gilmer County. This was the year General Winfield Scott was charged with the removal of the Cherokee. The 1840 census lists only family members in the household.

Trammell had already visited household number 584, the home of John M.'s married brother Andrew J., thirty-two, and his wife Harriet, twenty-four. Having followed his father into metalwork, Andrew was a blacksmith. He was probably named for Andrew Jackson, who was elected president in 1828, the year Andrew was born in South Carolina. Ten days before, in the Edom district close by, Trammell had recorded another Douthit brother: Davis, twenty, at household 470, with his twenty-year-old wife Harriet, illiterate. [Warren] Davis Douthit, also listed as a "farm hand," owned no land and reported an estate of $300. Next to him lived Alfred Weaver and his wife Margaret Douthit Weaver, a first cousin of John, Davis, and their siblings. Alfred, too, was a farmer.

In 1860, most adult residents of Fannin County listed birthplaces in other states, primarily North Carolina, South Carolina, Tennessee, and Virginia; and many, but not all, were Scots-Irish farmers and merchants. John M. (our subject) and Martha Douthit, however, were both native north Georgians, born near where they lived in 1860. John M. was born on his parents' Georgia farm on July 21, 1837. Martha Emeline Willson was born not far away on the 17th of November to Thomas Alexander Willson and Mary Adeline Watts Willson.

Many years later, in 1956, Henry Clay Curtis, the son of Martha's sister Julietta Condecy (or Julitty as it was pronounced and often spelled in the family), published a Willson family history in *The Fannin County Times*. In it he stated that Martha's father, Thomas Willson, was one of the first three white men to settle in the area that would become Fannin County, the other two being Elijah Chastain and Ebenezer Witzel. Thomas Willson brought his wife Mary and son

4

Richard there from Buncombe County, North Carolina, in late summer or fall 1832. He drove a Schooner wagon to a five-hundred-acre section he had purchased on the Toccoa River. Cherokee neighbors helped him build a log cabin with a dirt floor. Julitty, who was five years younger than Martha, remembered their mother describing the Cherokee as friendly but given to petty thievery and threats when they wanted something the Willsons had. Thomas Willson learned to speak Cherokee and did some mission work among them. Like the Cherokee, the new settlers resided in log houses and raised their own vegetables as well as oats, corn, wheat, rye, and livestock. Sheep provided wool for clothing, and fish and game augmented their diet.[9]

Collateral relatives of our Douthit family also claimed to be the first to arrive in the future Fannin County. On their tombstones in Galloway Cemetery, William Frazier Galloway and Levisa McClure Galloway are declared to be the first white settlers. Levisa was the sister of Lilly Ann Douthit, John's mother. In 1860 the Galloways lived in the Pierceville district (household 555) next to their son William McDaniel Galloway, his wife, and their two-year-old daughter. A Galloway family history states that William Frazier Galloway "was assigned by Governor John Clark to travel to North Cherokee County as a blacksmith for the Cherokee Indians" and that he settled on Hot House Creek in 1822.[10]

In 1860 Martha's parents, Thomas and Mary Willson, still lived in the Hot House district (household 615) with their younger children as did her older brothers John Vandiver

---

[9] In 1956, Curtis published a twelve-part article on the Willson family, one part per week from April 27 to July 19, in *The Fannin County Times*. I also own a typescript.

[10] Quoted in Charles F. Galloway, "Galloway Family," in Ethelene Dyer Jones, ed., *Facets of Fannin: A History of Fannin County, Georgia* (Dallas, TX: Curtis Media Corp., 1989), 31.

(616) and Richard (665). Her uncle Levi Willson, Thomas's brother, lived in the Stock Hill district (898), near neighbors William A. Twiggs (783) and Benjamin Tilley (887). Other names in the census suggest an even tighter familial and neighborly network. For example, there are Elrods, a family that intermarried with the Douthits in North Carolina, and McClures, the maiden name of John M.'s mother Lilly. At household 663, two doors away from Martha's brother Richard, lived the Thomas Curtis family, which included three sons of military age. A man named Thomas F. Anderson lived with his wife and children at number 621. He would be drawn into the family as a result of the Civil War. In fact, what happened to the Douthits, Willsons, Curtises, Galloways, Andersons, and their neighbors in the war is a microcosm of what happened throughout the county, the state, and the nation.

The 1860 United States census presents a group portrait of its citizens and non-citizens on the eve of the greatest cataclysm ever to take place on US soil. In Fannin County, 5,139 inhabitants were counted, including 76 black males and 67 black females on the "slave schedule." Not one of those inhabitants could have foreseen the magnitude of suffering the population would endure before the next census would be recorded in 1870. In retrospect, they seem as innocent as a flock of flightless birds picking in a field, unaware that thousands of wolves are about to spring out of the surrounding forest and tear them apart: the wolves of war.

2

Gone for a Soldier

By early 1861, the dominoes of secession were falling fast in the South. In November 1860, the election of Abraham Lincoln had virtually assured war. South Carolina seceded from the Union in December. In January, Mississippi, Florida, Alabama, Georgia, and Louisiana followed. Texas departed the Union on February 1. That month the Provisional Confederate Congress convened in Montgomery, Alabama. On the 18th, Jefferson Davis was sworn in as President of the Confederacy, with Alexander Hamilton Stephens of Georgia as his Vice President. In the north, Lincoln was inaugurated on March 4. By the end of May, Virginia, Arkansas, Tennessee, and North Carolina had also seceded.

Most Georgians believed the war would be over in a few months, if not weeks. Patriotism ran high. Military veteran I. W. Avery later noted in his post-war history of Georgia, "During the year 1861, the military activity in the State of Georgia was incessant and ubiquitous. The commonwealth was one vast recruiting camp....The war spirit boomed like a storm. The rivalry to enlist was universal and unquenchable."[1] Governor Joseph Elisha Brown was responsible for much of

---

[1] I. W. Avery, *The History of the State of Georgia from 1850 to 1881, Embracing Three Important Epochs: The Decade Before the War; The War; The Period of Reconstruction, with Portraits of the Leading Public Men of This Era* (New York: Brown & Derby, 1881), 191.

that military activity. A popular lawyer and former teacher, he was pushing hard for secession, but he wanted to keep the troops he recruited close to home for defensive purposes. Prior to secession, he had begun expanding the Georgia militia. This move "would make Georgia militarily the best-prepared state in the Confederacy when fighting actually broke out."[2] In 1861 Brown also sent troops to occupy Ft. Pulaski in Savannah harbor and took over both the Federal Arsenal at Augusta and the Federal Mint at Dahlonega, in Lumpkin County.

Many in northeast Georgia, above the cotton belt and oriented commercially towards Union-leaning eastern Tennessee rather than the Deep South, were not anxious to join the Confederate cause; and this was particularly true of Fannin County. On May 1, 1861, the pro-Secessionist *Southern Watchman* newspaper of Athens invoked both the Auld Sod and the danger to Imperial Rome from invading northern barbarians in declaring,

> We have been sending on companies to meet the wants of the country. This process is too slow. Let us have a *regiment* in Northeastern Georgia—a regiment of the hardy, brave, and patriotic rural population of our country—aye, three or four of them for that matter....Where can better material be found for forming a No. 1 Regiment than in Northeastern Georgia? Not even the Highlands of Scotland can furnish braver or hardier men....We are threatened with invasion by overwhelming numbers from the North. Like the Huns, Goths, and Vandals, they threaten to over-run and desolate our land...."To arms! To arms! ye brave!"—Vindicate the rights of your section and protect your homes from the pollution of these Northern negro-worshippers, who want to elevate the negroes to an

---

[2] William R. Scaife and William Harris Bragg, *Joe Brown's Pets: The Georgia Militia 1861–1865* (Macon, GA: Mercer University Press, 2004), 3.

equality with the whites; and who, to do so, stand ready to burn your houses and devastate your country![3]

In March President Davis called for 100,000 volunteers to serve twelve months. On April 12, South Carolina fired on Fort Sumter, to which event President Lincoln responded with a call for 75,000 Federal troops to serve three months. Ten days later, men from Fannin County formed Company E of the 2nd Volunteer Infantry Regiment, signing up for twelve months. They named themselves the Joe Browns for the governor, who was from Union County on Fannin County's eastern border. Thomas Trammell, the census taker of 1860, was among the enlistees. On July 3 the 11th Volunteer Infantry Regiment, Company E, mustered in, calling themselves the Fannin Young Rifles. Company F of the 11th, Mrs. Joe Brown's Boys, mustered in the same day and took in John M.'s first cousin, William McDaniel Galloway. Neighboring Lumpkin County provided two companies as well.

What did all this mean to young John Douthit on Hot House Creek? War was the main, unavoidable topic of conversation, but neither he nor his brothers leapt to enlist. John, Andrew, Solomon, and Davis were all of an age to enlist, but service and gratitude to country were strong presences in their lives and the South wanted to secede. The first John Douthit in their line, arriving in Philadelphia from Ireland in 1724 with his parents, was a Quaker who became allied with the pacifist Moravians in North Carolina. He did not serve in the American Revolution but supplied wheat to the Continental Army. Today, a DAR plaque marks his grave in Forsyth County. Men in the next generation of Douthits served in the War of 1812. Both Andrew and Solomon were old enough to remember the removal of the Cherokee from northeast Geor-

---

[3] *Southern Watchman* (Athens, GA) 8/5, (1 May 1861): 3.

gia by the US military; the family owed their land to President Jackson's actions against Native Americans. Further, Fannin County was named for a military hero, James Walker Fannin, Jr., who died in the Goliad Massacre during the Mexican War. On the other hand, the Fannin County Douthits probably knew that cousins in Georgia, South Carolina, and Tennessee were signing up to fight for the Confederacy.

On August 8, the Confederate government passed another recruitment act, asking for volunteers "not exceeding four hundred thousand" to serve for "not less than twelve months or more than three years."[4] The number alone must have been sobering to those not yet committed.

Still, by September only 25 percent of eligible Fannin County men had answered the call,[5] and now a new problem arose: the war was not over. Early recruits to Governor Brown's First Georgia Regulars had signed up for six months and Confederate Army recruits for twelve months. News from the Army of Virginia, to which the early north Georgia companies, including the 11th Infantry Regiment, had been sent, told of victories, to be sure, but also of local men maimed and killed. As Albert Moore notes of those Georgia troops, "Contemplating a short war, they had rushed off madly to the battlefront without making provisions for the care of their families. They felt that they should at least have a month or two in which to go home and adjust matters there, and many of them felt that it was only just that they should retire and let those

---

[4] James M. Matthews, ed., *The Statutes at Large of the Provisional Government of the Confederate States of America from the Institution of the Government February 8, 1861, to its Termination, February 18, 1862, Inclusive* (Richmond, VA: R.M. Smith, 1864), 176.

[5] Jonathan Dean Sarris, *A Separate Civil War: Communities in Conflict in the Mountain South* (Charlottesville, VA: University of Virginia Press, 2006), 52.

who had not yet served have their turn."[6] Besides, on the home front, tensions were increasing between the "secesh" proponents and the Tories, or Union sympathizers. Staying home to protect one's family from invasion and from partisan neighbors contended with joining the Army to protect the greater South, as the war propaganda urged.

On September 10, a call for volunteers was held in militia district 1029, the Hot House area. Ninety-eight able-bodied men between the ages of eighteen and forty-five were inscribed on the roll, including John's brothers Andrew and Solomon but not John or his brother Davis.[7]

Like many young family men, John would have been reluctant to leave his wife and baby daughter, the small farm that was his livelihood, and his widowed mother and siblings next door. As Jonathan Sarris observes, "The overwhelming majority of Fannin residents were farmers, either working their own land or that of others....Many had immigrated [sic] from North Carolina or Tennessee, seeking the Jeffersonian dream of self-sufficiency and economic independence."[8] Moreover, from the beginning of the turmoil, the concept of states' rights, used to sell the rebellion, collided with allegiance to a new central government. Many Southerners soon saw that the Confederacy was setting up its own central government to assert authority over its citizens, much like the government in Washington. Governor Brown was in favor of secession but was also a fierce advocate of states' rights and a thorn in the side of Jefferson Davis on that topic for most of the war. There is no evidence that John or his family knew the gover-

---

[6] Albert Burton Moore, *Conscription and Conflict in the Confederacy* (New York: Macmillan Co., 1924), 19.

[7] Handwritten muster roll, district 1029, Fannin County GA, courthouse records, unpaged.

[8] Sarris, *A Separate Civil War*, 37.

nor personally, but the Browns came from Londonderry in Ireland, as did the Douthits. Further, both families had lived in the Pickens District of South Carolina before coming to north Georgia. So John might have felt a kinship with the governor that eventually influenced him towards signing up for service and, at the same time, complicated his loyalties.

John's own family, like so many in the region, had split allegiances. His wife's nephew Henry Clay Curtis, tellingly named after the Great Compromiser who hoped to avoid a war between the states, recalled that the Willsons, Martha's family, were anti-slavery, anti-secession, and anti-war.[9] John Vandiver Willson, Martha's brother, would eventually "refugee" to Tennessee and join the 11th Tennessee Cavalry USA. In general, northeastern Georgians had little personal stake in preserving slavery or enriching cotton planters. Alexander Stephens's Cornerstone Speech, delivered March 21, 1861, had placed the perpetuation of slavery firmly in the center of the argument for secession. But although the Fannin County Douthits did not own enslaved people in 1860, the family had experience with slavery. John M. never showed support or opposition to it in his letters, but his grandfather Solomon Douthit had owned enslaved people in South Carolina, and his father, as has been noted, listed one male and one female in his possession on the 1830 census when the family lived in McMinn County, Tennessee, just prior to their move to Georgia. Other issues of economics and self-determination were also in play, including fear of invasion by northern troops on the one hand and resentment toward the political power of the wealthy on the other. "For North Georgians," Sarris concludes, "loyalty would remain ambiguous and contingent."[10]

---

[9] Curtis, Willson family story typescript, 7.
[10] Sarris, *A Separate Civil War*, 51.

Meanwhile, the need for recruits increased, as did the pressure to enlist. The loyalty and bravery of north Georgians, in particular, was being called into question, and its men wanted to prove they were both loyal and courageous. In December, to sweeten the deal for enlistees, the Confederate government, now in Richmond, offered a $50 bounty in exchange for reenlistment, a sixty-day furlough, and the right of soldiers to form units and elect officers. Almost immediately these bonuses were extended to new recruits.

In early 1862, a series of defeats deflated the South's initial confidence. In January, the Union prevailed at the Battle of Mill Springs in Kentucky, and the Confederate leader, Felix Zollicoffer, was killed there. The next month, Confederate-held forts Henry and Donelson fell in Tennessee. Virginia's Roanoke Island was captured. A huge cache of supplies for Georgia and Virginia troops was destroyed in Nashville. After Fort Sumter, the Union had blockaded southern ports. Certain goods began to be scarce. In a letter published in the *Southern Confederacy* newspaper in March, Georgia State Senator Benjamin H. Hill urged a stiffer resistance but conceded, "Our great successes had made us too confident, and over confidence had rendered us too careless as a people. Roanoke and Donelson were needed to admonish us, and therefore they were sent."[11]

Although Governor Brown and Vice President Stephens, among others, were bitterly opposed to conscription, it was becoming clear that depending on volunteers alone would not produce the numbers needed to win the war. But how degrading it would be now to be forced to enlist, when so many friends and neighbors had joined up without coercion. And as Sarris points out, by the end of 1861, public feeling in Lump-

---

[11] *Southern Confederacy* (Atlanta) 2/20 (March 8, 1862): 2. Hill's letter was dated March 1.

kin and Fannin counties, which originally opposed secession, had changed. "In order to deflect charges of Unionism or disloyalty, mountain Georgians embarked on a concerted attempt to prove their loyalty to the Confederacy. Highlanders' battle to shape their public image would dominate local consciousness throughout the war years and after."[12] The threat of conscription, more than anything else, swelled the ranks of volunteers.

On March 4, 1862, at Morganton, the Fannin county seat, John M. Douthit enlisted as a private in the Confederate Army, eventually to serve in the 52nd Georgia Volunteer Infantry Regiment, Company H, named the Fannin Rifles. As the son of a gunsmith, he must have known something about firearms. Although Andrew, Solomon, and Warren Davis Douthit did not sign up with him, Alfred Weaver, the husband of his first cousin Margaret, joined, as did a number of acquaintances. One was Benjamin M. Tilley, who would later provide Martha with crucial information about John's fate at Vicksburg.

On March 8, John filed his will with the Fannin County court, leaving everything to Martha "so long as she remains a widow and at her Death then for my Children to have it."[13] Martha was four months pregnant with their second child. John's brothers Andrew and (Warren) Davis were witnesses, along with S. N. Garen (sic), no doubt a relative of Davis's wife Harriet Garren Douthit.

Perhaps John joined on the upswing of sentiment described in the *Southern Recorder* newspaper of Milledgeville on the very day of his enlistment, written to rally public feeling after the earlier losses: "...the call by the President for 100,000

---

[12] Sarris, *A Separate Civil War*, 45.
[13] "Miscellaneous 1858" volume at Blue Ridge Courthouse, Blue Ridge, GA, 312.

additional troops, and the activity which pervades the whole service to strike the foe wherever he may present himself, has not only reassured the minds of the people, but it has given two-fold vigor to our limbs, and new courage to our souls. What seemed at first a misfortune will prove a blessing in the end."[14]

On April 16, one month before the twelve-months' service of 148 Confederate regiments was set to expire, the Confederate legislature passed the First Conscription Act. Every able-bodied white man between eighteen and thirty-five, eligible for military service, was drafted for three years or until the war was over, unless exempted. By then, John had left home with his unit. He was one among some 60,000 troops, according to Governor Brown's estimate, that Georgia provided to the Confederacy by April 1862.

The early enthusiasm for war would be short-lived among many ordinary Georgians. More than half of the white population in the South had not wanted immediate secession, but the issue was never submitted to the popular vote in any of the seceding states. In Georgia, 87 percent of the delegates to the secession convention were planters,[15] and Governor Brown lied about the number of votes that selected the delegates.[16] The "plain folk" would soon begin to question why their sacrifices for the cause were so much greater than those of the elites and would come to resent the unfairness of the war effort and the concomitant suffering of their families.

---

[14] "The South Waking Up," *Southern Recorder* (Milledgeville, GA) 43/9 (March 4, 1862): 3.

[15] David Williams, Teresa Crisp Williams, and David Carlson, *Plain Folk in a Rich Man's War: Class and Dissent in Confederate Georgia* (Gainesville, FL: University Press of Florida, 2002), 15.

[16] Williams et al., *Plain Folk in a Rich Man's War*, 20.

3

Camp McDonald

In early 1862, Wier Boyd, a prominent attorney in Dahlonega and a veteran of the Second Seminole War, traveled the northeastern Georgia counties to raise a regiment for the Confederacy. It was this regiment, the Georgia 52nd Volunteer Infantry Regiment, that John and others from Fannin County joined when they enlisted in March, and they proceeded to Camp McDonald for training. Immediately they got a taste of the excitement, but also the hardships, to come. As William S. Kinsland describes it,

> They came down from the isolated little communities in the hills of Habersham County, from the gold mines of Lumpkin County, from the copper mines and mills of Fannin County, and from the cabins and farms of Dawson, White, Franklin, Towns, Union and Rabun Counties. They all came together and marched from the old rallying places of former wars like the Dahlonega Mustering Grounds and the Denton Springs Mustering Ground and elsewhere. In the early spring of 1862, these men marched down from the mountains in the midst of torrential rainstorms, crossing swollen rivers and trudging through mud by day and sleeping in rain-soaked haystacks by night.[1]

Nor were their troubles over when they reached camp near Big Shanty (now Kennesaw) on Thursday, March 13. In

---

[1] William S. Kinsland, "The 52nd Regiment, Georgia Infantry," *North Georgia Journal* 2/2 (summer 1985): 10.

a letter written to his wife Sarah, Wier Boyd said, "We arrived safely at Camp McDonald on Thursday last amid great storms of rain. The authority had no tents for us and we, with several other companies from our region, stopped east of Camp McDonald some 2 miles."[2]

Camp McDonald, the largest training camp for the Georgia military in the Civil War, opened on June 11, 1861. Situated along the Western & Atlantic Railroad, encompassing streams and springs, and taking in grounds of the Georgia Military Institute, the camp offered sixty days of training under the instruction of GMI cadets. The town, Big Shanty, was named for the shanties that housed workers during the construction of the railroad. It was on a "big grade" leading from the Etowah River, hence Big Shanty.

The preserved correspondence of John M. Douthit begins at Camp McDonald. His first letter sets the tone for the rest. He is calm and inclined to take things as they come. Perhaps his attitude partly stems from a desire not to worry Martha and disturb her pregnancy.

Camp McDonald March the 22 the 1862
Dear Martha
I now take my pen in hand to write you a few lines to let you know that I am well at this time hoping they may come to hand and find you all well we reached this place on Sunday after we left Morganton on Wednesday and found the hills covere[3] with tents and soldiers, we elected our officers day before yesterday Boyed of Lumpkin is

---

[2] Quoted in Kinsland, "The 52nd Regiment," 10.
[3] I have tried to reproduce John's letters as he wrote them, using his spellings and lack of paragraphing, occasionally providing correct spellings in brackets if his meaning is unclear. His use of punctuation is erratic, which may indicate that he was in a hurry or distressed.

colonel.[4] Phillips lieutenant colonel[5] Fenly[6] for Major we
have not been mustered in to servis yet but we will be in in
a day or two I am as well satisfied as I expected to be
though some of the boyes are very much dissatisfied with
the fare but I think we will have a plenty in a few day the
worst with me is in coocking it but I think we will soon be
better fixed with coock vessles we have beef and flour
some pork and some corn meal sugar and molasses there
now is six Regiments and a Battalion here at this time
there is some sickness in camps at this time some few cases of the measles but none in our company write to me as
soon as you can and tell me how you and all of the friends
are getting along give my respects to all inquiring friends
tell the boys to write to me so nothing more at this time
but remains your husband until death

John, M, Douthit

[page 2][7]

P.S. Direct your letter to Camp McDonald in care of
capt Brown[8] of the Fannin Rifles tell R. Willson[9] I received his letter this morning and will write to him as soon
as the boys gets their money

J, M, Douthit

Richard Willson, Martha's older brother, was a merchant.
It could be that some of John's fellow soldiers—and maybe he

---

[4] Wier G. Boyd (1820–1893). An attorney and state legislator, he was
born in Hall County, Georgia, and rose to prominence in Lumpkin County.

[5] Charles D. Phillips. Elected lieutenant-colonel, Phillips had enlisted
as a private in Company A.

[6] James Jefferson Findley (1829–1888) of Lumpkin County.

[7] John is inconsistent in numbering his pages. Page numbers supplied
by the transcriber are indicated by brackets.

[8] William W. Brown, captain of the Georgia 52nd, Company H.

[9] Richard Willson (1831–1909), who lived in Fannin County at this
time.

himself—outfitted themselves on credit at Richard's store, promising to pay their bills when they received their $50 signing bonus. Enlistees counted on the army supplying their needs once they got to camp and probably brought little with them. In presenting the muster roll for the 2nd Infantry Regiment Company E (the "Joe Browns") the previous April, Captain W. A. Campbell included a letter explaining for his Fannin County recruits, "We have no arms, tents or camp furniture. In fact all that we have, is 65 men rank & file & all have one good substantial suit of clothes but not all alike and one change of underclothing. We will expect to be supplied by the state...my company prefer Sharps' rifles."[10] A disturbing coda to the availability of firearms is reported in *Plain Folk in a Rich Man's War*: "...class disparity became clear early on when the Confederate government, lacking weapons enough for all its volunteers, allowed those who could provide their own to enlist for only one year instead of three. Most volunteers were not informed until they reached the front lines that their shotguns and squirrel rifles would not do for military service."[11]

The regiments that eventually made up the brigade in which John served for his entire tenure, the 40th, 41st, 42nd, 43rd, and 52nd Volunteer Infantry Regiments, all trained at Camp McDonald. Once the brigade achieved its final form, it would number 6,769 men and be placed first under the command of General Seth Barton and later under General Marcellus Stovall. Because they had volunteered, these men were allowed to serve with others from their home counties and to elect officers. The elected officers at this time in the Civil War, in comparison to the rank and file, were men of wealth and position. Some, such as Wier Boyd, would attain high po-

---

[10] Capt. W. A. Campbell to Henry C. Wayne, Adjutant General, 24 April 1862, Confederate Service Records, National Archives.

[11] Williams et al., *Plain Folk in a Rich Man's War*, 23.

litical office. James Jefferson Findley was a slaveholder who owned a gold mine in Lumpkin County. After resigning from the 52nd, he would become a militia leader on the home front. Others commissioned as officers at Camp McDonald already had personal connections within the military. For example, Lieutenant Colonel Charles Phillips was the brother of Colonel William Phillips, who commanded Phillips' Legion with distinction in Virginia. William Phillips had named Camp McDonald after his law mentor, Governor Charles McDonald. Wier Boyd's son, seventeen-year-old Gus (Augustus), left Phillips' Legion and came to Camp McDonald to serve under his father, who appointed him Sergeant Major.

In a letter to his wife written March 16, Private Leander F. Crumley of the 52nd Company B (the "Cleveland Volunteers" of White County) noted that Governor Brown had visited the troops. Crumley corroborated John's report of cooking woes: "We have bad chance about cooking; as we have only one water bucket, one sheet iron bucket that we boil in, one frying pan and two coffee pots and three tin cups to cook with."[12] In a letter dated March 29, Crumley stated that the regiment still had no blankets and that it had snowed. He advised his wife to get started making woolen cloth as soon after sheep-shearing time as possible so that she could make his uniform and save him from having to buy one. In his letter of April 13, he appeared to reference a clothing allowance, of which he had spent $15.80 to get "coat, pants, caps, shirts, draws [sic] and shoes."

The camp sickness John mentions began to claim lives. In his March 29 letter, Crumley named two acquaintances who

---

[12] Leander F. Crumley, letters to wife Nancy E. Crumley, dated March 16, March 29, April 6, and April 13, 1862. Scans of originals and transcriptions found here: files.usgarchives.net/ga/Madison/history/letters/crumley.

had died and noted that he himself had a bad cold. On April 6, he wrote of three more deaths in camp as well as five desertions and remarked, "...this is no place for a sick man." The sicknesses would accelerate in lethal effect. Men coming from remote farms and mountain communities, where they had little exposure to disease, were mortally vulnerable even to childhood illnesses. In fact, the governor himself caught the mumps on a May visit to Camp McDonald. The mumps turned into a "slow fever."[13]

The new recruits were kept busy. In his history of the Campbell Salt Springs Guards, Mitchell Kelley describes the schedule at Camp McDonald:

> A drum roll sounded at 5:00 a.m., signaling the start of the day. Within an hour, breakfast was prepared and eaten. Following common practice, groups of four to ten soldiers would form a mess, whereby food and duties for cooking and cleaning were rotated and *shared*. Often the soldiers who formed messes were linked by prior acquaintances or were related....Breakfast usually consisted of cornbread, or grits cooked or reheated in some fashion, and beef. Little or more often than not, no fruits were available. Coffee or its substitute—an amber mixture brewed from parched peanuts, potato skins, dried apples, corn or rye - was served hot.

> From 6:00 a.m. to 8:00 a.m., fatigue was undertaken to gather and clean equipment. At 8:00 a.m., guard was mounted for the next 24-hour period; with a rotation of two hours on and four off duty. For the remainder of the regiment, drill was practiced. At noon, lunch was prepared, again by the various messes. By 2:00 p.m., additional duties, such as instruction on firearms, bayonet and company level drill were assigned. At five o'clock, the entire regiment paraded before the camp commander fol-

---

[13] *Southern Confederacy* 2/88 (May 29, 1862): 3.

lowed by supper at 6:00 p.m. A meal frequently prepared was "cush". The recipe varied depending on what ingredients were on hand, yet for the most part, cush was prepared as follows: fried bacon or cut cold beef was dipped into hot grease, water was added and the entire mixture stewed into a hash. Cornbread was crumbled into the stew and simmered until hot. Rice, peanuts, roasted corn, and field peas occasionally rounded out the meal. If available, molasses or sugar sweetened the servings of cush. Finally, coffee or its substitute was prepared. From 7:00 p.m. until 9:00 p.m., soldiers visited, wrote letters, sang, smoked or read. A long drum roll marked the end of the day at nine o'clock. This routine was practiced without variation for the entire time Company K stayed at Camp McDonald, which turned out to be less than a full month.[14]

After John's March 22 letter, the next letter we have is dated June 7. This gap may be the first indication that not all of John's letters have survived. It is unlikely he failed to write about the stunning event that occurred at Big Shanty between those dates. Leander Crumley told all about it in his April 16 letter to his wife. Among Douthit descendants, the story was passed down that John was present at the beginning of the Great Locomotive Chase.

Around 5 a.m. on April 12 at the train station in Marietta, a few miles away, a group of men boarded the northbound Atlanta-Chattanooga train. Union soldiers disguised in civilian clothes bought tickets separately so as not to attract attention. Led by one James Andrews of Flemingsburg, Kentucky, they would be known to history as Andrews' Raiders. Their mission was to steal "the General," the locomotive of that

---

[14] Mitchell Kelley, "The Campbell Salt Springs Guards: A History of Company K, 41st Regiment, Georgia Volunteer Infantry, Army of Tennessee, CSA," available at http://www.rootsweb.ancestry.com/~gacampbe/ Company_K_History.htm.

train, and ride it to Chattanooga and into Union territory, tearing up track and destroying bridges and telegraph lines along the way.

At Big Shanty, the train was scheduled to stop so that passengers and crew could breakfast at the Lacy Hotel. Why the Raiders chose that place to make their move is explained in a book written by William Pittenger, an Ohio soldier who volunteered for the caper. He also offered another origin of the name "Big Shanty:"

> It was a thrilling moment when the conductor called out, "Big Shanty! Twenty minutes for breakfast!" and we could see the white tents of the rebel troops and even the guards slowly pacing their beats. Big Shanty (now called Kenesaw) had been selected for the seizure because it was a breakfast station, and because it had no telegraph office. When Andrews had been here on the previous expedition, few troops were seen, but the number was now greatly increased. It is difficult to tell just how many were actually here, for they were constantly coming and going; but there seems to have been three or four regiments, numbering not far from a thousand men each. They were encamped almost entirely on the west side of the road, but their camp guard included the railroad depot. As soon as the train stopped, the conductor, engineer, fireman, and most of the passengers hurried for breakfast into the long low shed on the east side of the road, which gave the place its name.[15]

Shortly after this, the soldiers on guard saw four men calmly climbing in the engine and assumed they were on legitimate railroad business. But conductor William Fuller, who happened to look out the window as he was breakfasting and

---

[15] William Pittenger, *Daring and Suffering: A History of the Andrews Raid into Georgia in 1862* (New York: The War Publishing Company, 1887), 103.

24

saw his engine moving away with but one car coupled to it, thought otherwise. Because of the impending Conscription Act, Fuller had been warned to watch for reluctant new recruits who would try to flee Camp McDonald by train. His first thought was that the General had been commandeered by conscripts who would abandon it as soon as they were clear of camp. Accordingly, he sprang up and pursued his engine on foot, expecting to reclaim it soon and lose little time on his schedule. He did have the foresight to send an associate back to Marietta, with orders to telegraph up the line in case something else was brewing. The Raiders were cutting the telegraph wires as part of their plan of destruction, but half a message did get through to Chattanooga, where they were headed. Still, thanks to the glib Andrews, who managed to talk his way past several stations by saying that the General had been pressed into service to take ammunition to General Pemberton's Rebel troops, the Raiders were not caught until Ringgold, nearly to Chattanooga, when they ran out of fuel and water.

Officer Charles Phillips of the 52nd joined the pursuing party that eventually recovered the engine and captured most of the Raiders.[16] Leander Crumley claimed a larger role for the 52nd: "...our Rigment has taken seven of the clan prisners and two more come in last night or rather yesterday evening and I havn't larnt whether our Rigment taken them or not which makes 9 in all that has bin taken...."[17] Eight raiders, including Andrews, were hanged; two escaped across Union lines; six escaped after capture; and six, including Pittenger, were released in a prisoner exchange in March 1863.

The day after the raid, April 13, John and his company received uniforms and the fifty-dollar bounty they were prom-

[16] *Southern Confederacy* 2/52 (April 15, 1862): 2.
[17] Crumley, letter, April 16, 1862.

ised when they enlisted on March 4. A March 28 letter from
the Confederate government in Richmond, Virginia, to Major
General Edmund Kirby Smith[18] in Knoxville had informed
Smith that the 39th, 40th, 41st, 42nd, 43rd, and 52nd Georgia Regiments, along with the 9th Battalion Georgia Volunteers, had been ordered to report to him in Knoxville,[19] where
troops were sorely needed. On April 8, Confederate President
Jefferson Davis had declared martial law in the Department of
East Tennessee, suspended the writ of *habeas corpus*, and
placed Major-General Smith in charge of the area.[20] In eastern
Tennessee the men from Georgia would find a situation of
divided loyalties much like that in John's home county. Many
citizens were Union sympathizers.

On April 17, the Georgia regiments with which John
would be associated for his entire stay in the military proceeded north to Dalton, Georgia, by rail[21] on their way to Camp
Van Dorn in Knoxville. Knoxville, situated on the Tennessee
River, four miles from the confluence of the French Broad and
Holston rivers, was home to around 3,700 people in 1860.
Knox Countians numbered 20,000 white people and 2,000
enslaved people. Robert E. Lee had ordered Smith to protect
the railroads of eastern Tennessee and Virginia. This meant

---

[18] Smith (1824–1893), a West Pointer and Mexican War veteran, was
then commander of the Army of East Tennessee. He would head the
Trans-Mississippi Department after Vicksburg fell and would surrender in
Texas at the end of the war. Subsequently, he taught mathematics and
botany at the University of the South.

[19] *The War of the Rebellion: A Compilation of the Official Records of the
Union and Confederate Armies* (Washington: Government Printing Office,
1884), ser. 1, vol. 10, pt. 2, 370. Hereafter this source will be designated as
OR.

[20] Doc. 141. Eastern Tennessee. Jefferson Davis's Proclamation. *Rebellion Record; a Diary of American Events*, vol. 4, ed. Frank Moore (New
York: D. Van Nostrand, 1865), 501.

[21] Crumley, letter, April 19, 1862.

Smith and his troops would be drawn into the struggle for Cumberland Gap, some sixty miles to the north, and for Kentucky.

4

Minding the Gap

John's next letter to Martha was sent from Knoxville in early June, shortly after his arrival there. Other soldiers from the north Georgia regiments had arrived in east Tennessee in April. The question arises, why did John arrive in Knoxville so late?

The regiments formed at Camp McDonald did not all travel together. Private Henry W. Robinson of the Georgia 42nd, for example, wrote to his wife Elizabeth from Bean Station near Morristown, Tennessee, as early as April 6.[1] After a few days in Dalton, Georgia, the men of the 52nd were sent on to Chattanooga without the motley weapons brought from home—squirrel rifles, rifles of Revolutionary War vintage—which they were instructed to leave behind. In Chattanooga they were provisioned with twelve boxes of new Enfield rifles from England, intended for Governor Brown's Georgia state militia but confiscated from the *CSS Nashville* by Confederate ordnance officers for distribution to General Kirby Smith's troops. When the Governor protested, he was assured that the rifles were "to be placed in the hands of the Fifty-Second

---

[1] Henry W. Robinson letter collection, Stuart A. Rose Manuscript, Archives and Rare Book Library, Emory University. Robinson uses formulaic greetings and farewells similar to those that John uses.

Georgia Regiment, [who were] at Chattanooga without arms."[2]

A letter from Private Crumley of the 52nd, company B, states that he arrived at Knoxville's Camp Van Dorn on April 18, after a direct twenty-two-hour train trip from Camp McDonald. "We had a pleasant ride if you call sitting on a rough plank a day and night anything," he remarked. Measles and mumps were tearing through camp, and he indicated that thirteen of the regiment had been left behind in a hospital in Marietta.[3] A report of troop strength dated April 24 included the 52nd Georgia, "unarmed."[4] Was John one of the sick, which might account for his silence? Perhaps, but not all companies traveled at the same time because of train delays, the number of soldiers, and other transportation problems. There was one track for competing interests from Camp McDonald to Knoxville. In any case, April 27 found most of the 52nd at Camp Van Dorn with Colonel Boyd complaining that half the regiment was "yet unfit for duty" due to measles and other illnesses.[5] Men began to die in camp. Boyd himself would fall ill and go home, not returning until September. Private Robinson noted from "Nox" [Knox] County, "Tha have alarge brick house for a hosepittel & tha is about 50 in it and it out stinks a ded horse...."[6]

John arrived in Knoxville on June 5 and soon wrote this letter to his wife.

---

[2] J[osiah] Gorgas to Governor Brown, in Allen D. Candler, ed., *Confederate Records of the State of Georgia*, vol. 3 (Atlanta: C. P. Byrd, State Printer, 1910), 211–12.

[3] Crumley, letter, April 19, 1862.

[4] *OR* series 1, vol. 10, pt. 2, p. 476. Other Georgia and Tennessee regiments are described as "badly armed—country rifles," "effective strength," and "partly and badly armed—country shot-guns."

[5] Quoted in Kinsland, "The 52nd Regiment," 12.

[6] Robinson, letter, April 17, 1862.

1862 Camp Vandorn, Knoxville Tenn June 7
    Dear Companion I now take the opportunity to write you a few lines to let you know that I am well at this time hoping that these few lines will come safe to hand and find you all well I reached this this [sic] place Thursday evning the Regiment is at Deep creek gap there is ten or fifteen of my company here that is unable for duty I do not know when I shall go to the Regiment but not for several days I don't expect it is thought here that there will be a fight out there [erasure] be fore long—turn over—
    I do not know that I have any thing more to write. So I will close by signing my name your affectionate husband
                                                John, M, Douthit

The brevity of John's second letter—practically the 1862 equivalent of a text message—could mean that longer letters, which have been lost, preceded it. Or he may have been ill. Shorter letters sometimes indicate that he felt too bad to write or did not want to worry Martha as to his condition.
    The highway marker for Knoxville's Camp Van Dorn describes the place from which Confederate forays to defend the Gap and eastern Tennessee were launched in spring and summer 1862. The location of the camp, lost for decades, was found again by 40th Georgia descendant Gary Goodson, who campaigned to have a historical marker installed at the site. Placed off Western Avenue near the *Knoxville News-Sentinel* building, the marker was unveiled in 2007 and reads as follows:

Major General E. Kirby Smith of the Confederate Army established Camp Van Dorn 1.5 to 2 miles west of Knoxville Depot, near the banks of a little stream, Third Creek. It operated from March 28 through July 28, 1862. Most Georgia Confederate Infantry regiments, including the 37th, 39th, 40th and 52nd from Camp McDonald at "Big

Shanty," Georgia were here. Diseases decimated the ranks of the Ga. 40th and 52nd, killing 137. Most of these Confederate dead were buried in Bethel Cemetery here in Knoxville.

Initially, the north Georgia regiments that would become the Barton-Stovall Brigade were placed in several other brigades in the Army of East Tennessee: the 40th and 52nd went into Brigadier General Seth Barton's Fourth Brigade, the 42nd was tapped to serve under Brigadier General Carter L. Stevenson in the Second Brigade, and the 43rd was assigned to the First Brigade with Brigadier General Danville Leadbetter. The 41st was sent for a time to Mississippi. We are left to wonder whether John, during his stay at Camp Van Dorn, ever met up with a first cousin, also named John Douthit, who was serving in the 39th Georgia with Colonel A. W. Reynolds's Third Brigade. This John Douthit, son of John's Uncle Robert, had enlisted on March 4 in Ellijay, Georgia, the county seat of Gilmer County. Ellijay is about twenty miles from Morganton, where John mustered in. This cousin is not mentioned in surviving letters.

The "Deep Creek Gap" in John's June 7 letter refers to Big Creek Gap near LaFollette in Campbell County. Big Creek Gap is some thirty miles southwest of Cumberland Gap in the Powell Valley. Loftily called the Keystone of the Confederacy, the narrow defile was one of several gaps in the mountain chain that provided important alternatives to Cumberland Gap for both armies. It changed hands more than once during John's tenure in the area.

Skirmishes would occur June 10 at Wilson's Gap and Roger's Gap, followed by skirmishes art Big Creek Gap on June 11 and 12. Troops at Big Creek Gap would participate in an "action" on June 15, as Union troops under General George Washington Morgan, commander of the Army of the Ohio, moved south through the Cumberland Mountains, intent on taking Cumberland Gap.[7] However, even as John wrote, most of the 4,000 Confederate troops in the Powell Valley were being shifted to Chattanooga or Clinton in anticipation of a Federal move to take the former. General Kirby Smith's resources were stretched thin between "the two principal strategic points" of his department, Cumberland Gap and Chattanooga, 180 miles apart.[8] In a May 1 letter to George W. Randolph, Confederate Secretary of War, Georgia Governor Brown emphasized the dire consequences both for his state and for the cause if Chattanooga were lost: "If it is taken, the railroad bridges on both sides of it burned, we are cut off from the coal mines, and all our iron mills are stopped."[9] Replying to this plea the next day, Jefferson Davis discussed the deployment of the north Georgia regiments, which at some point he had meant to place in Chattanooga permanently: "I concur with you as to the importance of Chattanooga. The six regiments called from Camp McDonald were with difficulty armed. Every effort was made to do so, that they might serve to defend the country to which you refer. They were removed without previously consulting me, and I have not been able to supply their place."[10]

John does not record any familiarity with eastern Tennessee, and it is likely he never had occasion to go so far from home. In some ways it was not so different from north Georgia, being a rural area largely populated by small farmers and miners, and with a view of mountains. British citizen J. Gray Smith visited the area twenty years before and wrote, "East Tennessee greatly resembles the lower ranges and fertile val-

---

[7] *OR*, ser. 1, vol. 10, pt. 2, p. 51.
[8] *OR*, ser. 1, vol. 10, pt. 2, p. 597.
[9] Candler, *Confederate Records*, 203.
[10] Candler, *Confederate Records*, 205.

leys of the Alps, and it has often been called the American Switzerland."[11] Today, US Highway 11E follows the route the troops marched from Knoxville northeast to various assignments. They covered ten to twenty miles a day. The terrain has long rises and declines and is cut by ravines. They also used the rail line to Morristown.

The Reverend Thomas William Humes, a Knoxville native and slaveholder who stayed in the city during the war, traced east Tennessee's anti-secessionist leanings to its early history. Despite the region's being linked only to slave states by rail and despite being distant from Union states, he said, the people "set their faces as a flint against secession," and not only because they had few enslaved people and grew cotton largely for personal use.[12] They also had a history of loyalty to the US government and of a desire to be part of the Republic, first through the establishment of the Wautauga Association, which provided rudimentary governmental services well before Tennessee became a state and produced the first constitution west of the Appalachians in 1772; then through the participation of East Tennesseans in the Battle of Kings Mountain against the British in 1780; and finally through the attempt to form the state of Franklin, which petitioned Washington for statehood in 1784. These initiatives, said Humes, showed "the same broad patriotism" that he found among the people at the start of the Civil War.[13] His view is still useful today, though Noel Fisher, for example, presents a much more nuanced view of east Tennessee Unionism.[14]

---

[11] Quoted in Thomas William Humes, *The Loyal Mountaineers of Tennessee* (Knoxville: Ogden Brothers & Co., 1888), 24.

[12] Humes, *Loyal Mountaineers*, 7.

[13] Humes, *Loyal Mountaineers*, 7.

[14] See Noel C. Fisher, *War at Every Door: Partisan Politics & Guerrilla Violence in East Tennessee 1860–1869* (Chapel Hill: University of North Carolina Press, 1997).

East Tennessee was so sympathetic to the Union that in 1861 it had held conventions with the aim of forming its own state. The vitriolic anti-secessionist newspaper editor, William "Parson" Brownlow, had challenged Confederate interests in Knoxville and had helped to harden opposing positions. So the Confederate regiments arrived into a fluid political situation and were seen as invaders, not saviors, by much of the populace. Among other duties, they were to round up those suspected of treason.

It has been said that the Rebel troops looked down on the people of eastern Tennessee, considering them less educated and less socially evolved than themselves. In the case of the north Georgia farmers, this is absurd, since they came from the same stock and lived the same kind of life. The superior air originated in a difference in loyalties, as *Southern Confederacy* correspondent T.D.W demonstrated in a letter published August 9, 1862:

Morristown, Tenn., Aug. 4, 1862

Dear Confederacy: ...I have noticed, during my stay in East Tennessee, one remarkable fact: that *ignorance* of the masses is the primary cause of all the toryism in this section. Nearly all of the respectable and well informed are true to the South. In no instance have I found an educated gentleman, or one who has much at stake, a follower of Lincoln. This must be, then, the effects of education. I find here more or less of the class called superstitious. They see ghosts, hobgoblins, trees on fire in the heavens, stars falling, worlds burning up, and a thousand other illusions that portend a large development of the supernatural.... If a cock comes in the house and gives a lively crow, straightway it is announced that a stranger is coming that very day. Horse shoes are abundant over the doors, and on inquiry I found it to mean the frightening off of witches. I find but few schools—few churches, and an enlightened gospel is seldom, if ever, heard in the mountains. This, then, is the truth of the whole matter: *ignorance and super-stition.* Follow the chain of mountains, even in Virginia and North Carolina, and as the people in and on the mountains are more or less ignorant, unrefined and super-stitious, the demagogue seeking an office finds his victims, and appeals to them by placing himself on a level with them... T. D. W.[15]

Nevertheless, the soldiers did mingle in quite a friendly fashion with the locals. From Bean Station, Private Robinson declared, "...if we Stay heare much longer in about 9 months from now thare will be more little Gorgians a Squalling through this contry then you can Shake a Stick at but I don't in tend to be cald pap so fare from home...."[16]

Soon John wrote again, with more detail. "Julitty," of course, is their daughter Julietta, who would turn two in August.

June 16th 1862
[illegible] Station Tenn
Dear Companion
    I now take this opportunity to drop you afew lines which will inform you that I am in tolerable health hoping these lines will come to hand and find you all well I will give you a small sketch of our travels for the past week as this is the first opportunity I had had to write. The Regiment came to Knoxville on Monday after I got here a Thursday on there way to Chattanooga we supposed we stoped at charlston on the Hiwassee River we stayed there two days and then we went back to Knoxville from thence we started to Cumberland gap so we had to take it on foot.

---

[15] "T.D.W.," *Southern Confederacy* 2/149 (August 9, 1862): 2.
[16] Robinson, letter to wife Elizabeth, August 3, 1862.

[page 2]
So we marched three days and got within five miles
of the gap and was turned back this morning which makes
the fourth day that we have been on the march and are all
nearly tired down though I have stood it a great deal better than I expected I would we are on our way to Chattanooga at this time but do not know how far we will get
until we are ordered to some other place so write often as
you can for it it [sic] uncertain about getting letters here as
we are moving constantly I am anxious to hear from you
and want to see Julitty very bad. So nothing more at present but remains your husband until death
John M, Douthit
Direct your letters to Knoxville Tenn.

The illegible address looks most like *Jones* Station. A place
by that name, now gone, was located in Hamilton County,
Tennessee. This makes sense, given John's description of his
journey from Knoxville to Chattanooga, the Hamilton County
seat. One wonders if John and his fellow soldiers knew that
Charleston was the staging area for the Cherokee Removal of
1838. Fort Cass was headquarters for General Winfield Scott,
who was in charge of the removal, and thousands of Cherokees were collected in the valley prior to setting out on the
Trail of Tears. Several hundred died before departure and are
buried in the area.[17]

Cumberland Gap, an opening in the 131-mile long Cumberland Mountain range near where Kentucky, Tennessee,
and Virginia come together, was a prize sought by both the
Confederacy and the Union. Confederate control could open
politically neutral Kentucky to a Rebel invasion from the

[17] Vicki Rozema, *Footsteps of the Cherokees: A Guide to the Eastern
Homelands of the Cherokee Nation* (Winston-Salem, NC: John F. Blair,
2000) 101–107.

South. Confederate generals Humphrey Marshall and Braxton Bragg, among others, believed that eastern Kentucky citizens would flock to join the invading forces, followed by the rest of the state. For their part, the Union sought to liberate Unionist eastern Tennessee from Confederate rule and open a route to Georgia. Whoever controlled Kentucky and Tennessee would also rule the Ohio River and the upper Mississippi.

B. F. Stevenson, a surgeon with the 22nd Kentucky Volunteer Infantry (Union) who was stationed at the Gap while the Federals occupied it, published this description after the War:

> [The Gap is] so narrow that wagons descending either way lock wheels on the same level space....The pinnacles on either side, clearly defined and in bold relief, stand in bleak and barren grandeur and desolation, having been almost entirely denuded of forest and shrub in obedience to military necessity. Huge masses of sandstone lie scattered in promiscuous confusion over the surrounding surface.... The roads from the valleys on either side wind and zigzag their way up the eleven hundred feet of elevation to reach the Gap, and are commanded throughout by earthwork fortresses erected at appropriate positions on the heights above.[18]

The same advantages that caused favorable comparisons with the defensive positions of Thermopylae and Gibraltar also made the Gap difficult to occupy for long. This pass, used by Dr. Thomas Walker, Daniel Boone, and others to bring settlers across the Appalachian Mountains via the Wilderness Road, was hard to supply. The rugged terrain made access dif-

---

[18] B. F. Stevenson, "Cumberland Gap: a paper read before the Ohio commandery of the military order of the Loyal Legion of the United States, June 3, 1885, by companion B.F. Stevenson, late Surgeon (Major) 22nd Kentucky Volunteer Infantry" (Cincinnati: H.C. Sherick & Co., 1885), 10.

ficult for assailants and defenders alike; and because the surrounding population was sparse and already poor, foraging by
soldiers from both armies soon exhausted the food and other
necessities in the countryside and on the local farms. The
Wilderness Road itself was hard to negotiate because of ravines and creeks that crossed it. Many pioneer families on
their way farther west gave up and settled in Tennessee's Powell Valley south of the Gap, where the Georgia troops now
were stationed.[19]

In May, Major Raleigh Camp of the Georgia 40th wrote
that his regiment and the 52nd were stationed for a month at
Big Creek Gap, on a major road linking east Tennessee to
Kentucky (today that road is US 25E). Kirby Smith arrived
and the men scouted here and there without engaging the enemy, moving from Big Creek Gap to Woodson's Gap to Wilson's Gap to Childreth's Gap to Baptist Gap along the Cumberland mountain chain. As Camp explained, "All our
marching up and down the Powell Valley was to check the
enemy from capturing Big Creek Gap, and thus cut off the
supply line to General Carter L. Stevenson[20] (Georgia 42nd)
at Cumberland Gap."[21] Seth Barton marched his men from
gap to gap in the mountains—there were seven small gaps between Cumberland Gap and Big Creek Gap alone—to make

---

[19] Federal Writers' Project, *The WPA Guide to Tennessee* (1939; repr.,
Knoxville, TN: University of Tennessee Press, 1986), 326.

[20] Brigadier General Carter Littlepage Stevenson, Jr. (1817–1888), a
West Point graduate from Virginia and veteran of the Second Seminole
War, the Mexican War, and of other service on the American frontier,
arrived in Tennessee in early 1862 to command a division under Edmund
Kirby Smith.

[21] Quoted in Gary Ray Goodson, Sr., "Part III—The Narrative,"
Georgia Confederate 7,000, (Shawnee, CO: Goodson Enterprises, 2000),
102.

the Federals think there were more Confederate troops guarding Tennessee than there were.

When John arrived in Knoxville, General Stevenson was in command of Cumberland Gap but under Federal pressure. The Rebels had occupied the Gap since mid 1861 when General Felix Zollicoffer cleared out the Home Guard and built fortifications on the north side to keep the Union from invading Tennessee. After he was killed at the Battle of Mill Springs on January 19, 1862, command of the Gap passed first to Colonel James E. Raines and then to General Stevenson. While Union General George W. Morgan was preparing an assault on the Gap from Kentucky, Federal troops approached Chattanooga to draw the Confederates away from the Gap. The Georgia troops were hurriedly sent south and John's regiment was put at Charleston, as he says, north of Chattanooga on the only rail line to Knoxville, to guard a bridge over the Hiwassee River. General Morgan wrote to General Buell on June 10, "The present fate of East Tennessee depends upon Kirby Smith being all occupied at Chattanooga."[22] When the Federals left Chattanooga and Morgan renewed his march towards the Gap, the Confederate troops were sent back to eastern Tennessee. Letters from other soldiers detail the number of sick or weary soldiers who had to be left behind at various stops. Some of the ill were sent back to Knoxville. At the same time, new recruits were brought out to the field. Again there was a shortage of tents and other supplies.

Meanwhile, behind Union lines, Private Robert Newton Gorsuch of the 16th Ohio Volunteer Infantry Company B was keeping a diary. On June 8 he wrote that his unit was camped fifteen miles from Wilson's Gap. The next day they crossed into Tennessee and on June 10 fired on Rebel cavalry. Gorsuch was on picket duty overlooking the Powell Valley and

---

[22] *OR*, ser. 1, vol. 10, pt. 1, p. 52.

guarding the road below when he wrote, "This is the most beautiful valley I ever saw. It is very level and smooth. I see wheat which will soon be fit to cut. I see negros working corn. Also houses, barns, green fields, and pieces of woodland here and there over the valley."[23] He was speaking of the Powell River Valley between the Gap and Knoxville. In the coming weeks, John would find himself marching all over this area, where skirmishes with the Federals broke out frequently. On Wednesday, June 11, Private Gorsuch noted, "The enemie's cavalry are gathered along the road in the valley. We can see them from the top of the mountain."[24] After his unit is ordered down into the valley, he says, "We are now between two forces of the enemy. There are 4,000 at Cumberland Gap and 3,000 at Big Creek Gap. They may attack us at night. But our brigade can whip any 7,000 rebels. 1 o'clock at night our pickets are firing like the duce."[25]

Between John's June 16 letter and the next one, an important event occurred. After a small Union force attacked Chattanooga, Stevenson was ordered to abandon the Gap and to destroy tents and guns there so Union troops could not use them. He did so June 16–18. The Georgia 40th and 52nd regiments, under General Barton, covered his retreat. T.D.W., the journalist for the *Southern Confederacy* embedded with the troops, wrote of the evacuation of the Gap, "As for myself, I was li[t]erally wearied of being in a country where the slightest movement was carried to our enemies the self same day; and

---

[23] Robert Newton Gorsuch, *Civil War Diaries and Selected Letters of Robert Newton Gorsuch (1839–1913)*, transcribed by Edith Irene Gorsuch Smith, Horace Greeley Smith, and Everett Gorsuch Smith, Jr. (privately printed, 2012), 55.

[24] Gorsuch, *Civil War Diaries and Selected Letters*, 56.

[25] Gorsuch, *Civil War Diaries and Selected Letters*, 56.

was glad when we left a border people that when help was of-fered them they would not aid themselves."[26]

On June 19, Private Gorsuch stated, "The enemy have left much property but destroyed it. They left several hundred tents but cut them to pieces. They left 5 cannons all 64 pounders."[27] On June 20 he recorded a move of his unit from Tennessee back into Kentucky, where he was sent out to for-age for berries.[28]

By June 21 the 52nd was back in Knoxville and had been transferred to Taylor's Brigade.[29] Private Crumley wrote home, "I don't know whether Taylor is a good General or not yet, but I know he can't make his men go through more than General Barton did."[30]

They did not stay in Knoxville long but proceeded to a settlement between the Holston and Clinch rivers at the base of Clinch Mountain. Within the straitjacket of epistolary for-mulas, John's next communication suggests another reason his letters were short and somewhat pro forma: his growing frus-tration at the lack of news from home.

> Blains Cross Roads
> June 24, 1862
> Dear Companion
> I again take the opportunity of dropping you a few lines to tell you that I am well at this time hoping these few lines will come to hand and find you all well I have

---

[26] "T.D.W.," *Southern Confederacy* 2/112 (June 26, 1862): 2.

[27] Gorsuch, *Civil War Diaries and Selected Letters*, 58.

[28] Gorsuch, *Civil War Diaries and Selected Letters*, 59.

[29] Thomas Hart Taylor (1825–1901). A native of Frankfort, Ken-tucky, Taylor was a cousin of President Zachary Taylor. Kirby Smith ap-pointed him to command the 5th Brigade of Stevenson's division. He was captured at Vicksburg and later released in a prisoner exchange.

[30] Crumley, letter, June 21, 1862.

nothing of interest to write you at this time We have left Knoxvill Wednesday morning and came to this place last night We do not know where we will go next but it is thought that we will go out to the Clinch mountains It is thought that there is a large force of the enemy of this side of the Cumberland mountains and if there is we will have some thing to do shortly but do not know the truth of the report I want you to be safe and write every week without fail

[page 2]

I am anxious to hear from you I have not heard from you since I left home I will write to you every week that is if I have the chance direct your letters to Knoxvill to Knoxvill [sic] nothing more at this timme

Your husband until death
John M Douthit

Blain's Crossroads, south of Clinch Mountain in Grainger County, is called Blaine today. The mountain range runs from near Blaine in a northeasterly direction up into Virginia. The regiment soon moved again.

June 28th 1862
Cedar fort Tenn

Dear Companion I again take my pen in hand to inform you that I am in tolerable health at this time hoping these lines will come to hand and find you all well I can say to you that I have not received neither letter nor any word from you since I left home I am very anxious to hear I can not give any reason for not getting letters from you as there has come letters to some of the boys mailed at Hot House the 25 of this month I have nothing of importance to write you at this time we are now twenty five miles from Knoxville between there and the Cumberland gap but do not know how long we will stay here but not long as we have to move every two or three days I thought

we would have had a fight but do not hear any talk of
fighting now I have no idea how many troups we have in
here
[page 2]
at this time but enough I think to whip as many of the enemy as will be sent over here there is Some sickness in
camps at this time and some deaths Rufus Pless[31] is dead
he died the 20 of this month there has been a few that has
died out of this company that we know of and three others
that we hear is dead but do not know whether it is so or
not So I must bring my letter to a close so nothing more at
this time but remains you husband until death John M.
Douthit

Send your letters to Knoxville Tenn in care of capt.
W W Brown 52 Reg't Ga Vol

Although John's letter clearly says "Cedar fort," such a
place cannot be found today. However, the town of Luttrell
lies twenty-two miles northeast of Knoxville, in the area John's
unit was crisscrossing. Until 1890 it was known as Cedar
Ford.

No letters from Martha survive, but one assumes she was
at least as diligent as he in corresponding. The Confederate
Postal Service, established February 21, 1861, with John H.
Reagan as Postmaster General, went through many adjust-
ments as US money and stamps were first used and then Confederate issue. Prices had to be standardized, routes manned,
and train service regularized. Shortages of ink and paper in the
South added to the difficulty of staying in touch. Because it
was hard to obtain stamps in war zones and on the march, letters from soldiers were eventually accepted without postage, as

---

[31] Private Henry R. Pless of Company H, who had enlisted with John
at Morganton, died of "fever" and was buried in Bethel Confederate
Cemetery in Knoxville.

John's next letter appears to indicate. The Confederate Post Office charged 5 cents ($1.14 in 2016 dollars) for sending letters up to 500 miles.[32] John and his fellows also entrusted letters to soldiers going home on furlough or to visitors returning home after seeing the troops. But constant troop movements and the destruction of rail lines by both sides complicated matters.

Camp near Cedar ford Tenn July the 3th 1862
Dear Companion, I again take my pen in hand to inform you that I am in tolerable health at this time hoping these few lines will come to hand and find you all well I received two letters from you on the 30th of June one dated 11th the other the 18th June and was very glad to hear from you and to hear that you was well you said that you wanted me to try and come home when you wrote for me to come I can say to you that I would gladly come at any time but there is no chance for a well man to go home they have sent most all the sick home that is able to get home there is agreat [sic] deal of news going at this time about the fight at Richmond the papers say that we have given them a terrible whipping there which I hope is so we are stationed 25 miles form [from] Knoxvill in avery [sic] pleasant cedar grove but do not know how long we will stay here. I do not think that we will have any fighting to do here shortly though I can't tell what may be done I want to see you all very bad but I do not know when I shall have the pleasure write to me every week and perhaps I will get a letter once and awhile and I will do the same if I can get paper I shall have to send this letter with out paing the postage for the want of stamps So nothing more at present but remains your husband until death

---

[32] "Mail Service and the Civil War," https://about.usps.com/news/national-releases/2012/pr12_civil-war-mail-history.pdf. Inflation numbers are based on the Consumer Price Index.

John M. Douthit.
Direct your letters to Knoxvill

The mention of Richmond must refer to General George B. McClellan's failed Peninsula Campaign. At this point many soldiers who were too sick to fight or march were being sent home. Others were deserting or not returning from furloughs, causing Colonel R. J. Henderson, commander of the Georgia 42nd, to run a notice in the *Southern Confederacy* newspaper of Atlanta, ordering those home on expired furloughs to rejoin the regiment immediately unless they could send "the certificate of a Physician of known representation and skill in his profession." Otherwise, the shirkers would be "brought back in chains, if necessary, by a squad of men detailed for that purpose, and tried as deserters."[33] A list of names was appended. The notice ran for weeks. At this time, the 42nd was in the Second Brigade of Stevenson's Division, under Colonel James E. Rains.[34] The Third, or Barton's Brigade, comprised the 30th and 31st Alabama infantry regiments, the Georgia 40th and 52nd, the 9th Georgia Battalion, and Captain J. W. Anderson's Battery. The Georgia 43rd was serving under Colonel A. W. Reynolds in the 4th Brigade.[35] The Georgia 41st, as noted, was in Mississippi.

John does not speak of troop discipline such as is mentioned above, but Private Robinson of the 42nd witnessed two sobering disciplinary events: a soldier executed by firing squad because "he had causd a lutennent to be kild he had not kild him him self but causd it to be done...." The man was brought

---

[33] *Southern Confederacy* 2/130 (July 18, 1862): 3.

[34] James Edwards Rains (1833–1862). A Yale law graduate from Nashville, Tennessee, Rains commanded the garrison at Cumberland Gap during winter 1861–1862. He was killed at the Battle of Stones River on December 31, 1862.

[35] *OR*, ser. 1, vol. 16, pt. 2, p. 719.

to the execution site seated on his own coffin and shot by a firing squad. Robinson concluded defiantly, "...he had all chances to Run but the gard was cloce by but if it had bin a cace of mine tha would a had to a Shot me on the wing...."[36] In June, the brigade was called together to witness six prisoners "tha had De Serted & tha giv them 39 lashes on the bare back & drummed them out of Camps under the tune of yankey doodle...."[37]

Throughout his service, as was true of most of his fellow soldiers, John remained steadfast in his commitment to participate if able. The scarcity of complaints in his letters implies a certain ownership of his situation and loyalty to a shared mission. So far, he had been fortunate to stay out of the line of fire. But he was not out of immediate danger.

---

[36] Robinson, undated letter, 1862.
[37] Robinson, letter, 7 June 1862.

5

On Rising Ground

John's next letter found him seventeen miles from Knoxville at a village on the Holston River, ill and lonely for news, but bearing up.

> Hospital [illegible] No. 2
> Strawberry Plains July the 17th 1862
> Dear Companion, I again take my pen in hand to let you know how I am I can say to you that I think I am doing as well could be expected though very weak I think the fever is broke on me so with care I think I will be up shortly. We have Goodman to doctor us and he takes a heap of pains with us all I have not found the hospital to be such a bad place as some recommend it We have good straw beds on bunks and pillows white sheets and we are not allowed to eat any strong diet that is those that are taken much medicen I hope these lines will come to hand in due time and find you all well and doing well You can not imagine how bad I want to hear from you but it seems like I never shall hear any more Direct your letters to Strawbery Plains in the care of
> [page 2]
> Sergeon Goodman and I think I will get them if you see S.M. Douthit tell him I want him to write to me and to let me know how all the folks are and to write who has been conscribed and whether they have left any boddy or not and who has hid out give best respects to all inquiring

friends so I will come to a close so nothing more at present but remains your husband until death

John, M, Douthit.

John's illness could have been any one of a number of "camp fevers," that is, fevers contracted from association with fellow soldiers and from camp conditions: typhoid, typhus, pneumonia, scarlet fever, or another ailment. In many cases, it was only years after the war that researchers studying Civil War medical records were able to match up reported symptoms with correct diagnoses.

There were many contributing factors to soldiers' health besides a specific disease; for example, inadequate physical examinations that allowed unfit men into the army; troops from rural areas who had never been exposed to common diseases and thus were fatally vulnerable to otherwise survivable ailments (here one also thinks of Native American populations who were devastated by "new" diseases brought by explorers and colonists); the ignorance of some troops, who did not know how to take care of themselves; poor hygiene practices (latrines built near water supplies); insects and rodents; exposure; shortages of clothing and shoes; poor food; no food; and unrecognized psychological issues.[1]

Given the above, being in a hospital could itself be a risky proposition. Germ theory was not widely accepted in the States until after the war, so sometimes the treatment itself was fatal. As George Worthington Adams puts it, "The Civil War was fought in the very last years of the medical middle ages."[2] Surgeons and nurses did not wash their hands between

---

[1] H. H. Cunningham, *Doctors in Gray: The Confederate Medical Service* (Baton Rouge: Louisiana State University Press, 1993), 163–81.

[2] George Worthington Adams, "Confederate Medicine," *The Journal of Southern History* 6/2 (May 1940): 151.

patient treatments or sterilize equipment. Equally dangerous was the practice of assigning the less sick hospital patients to serve as nurses, in which capacity they both fed the bedridden and emptied bedpans and urinals without observing what we now accept as basic rules of sanitation.[3] After his illness waned, John appears to have stayed on to care for men in his regiment. H. H. Cunningham writes, "The great enervating ailments of the Southern fighting men were the intestinal disorders, diarrhea and dysentery,"[4] whatever was meant by those terms. Diarrhea could be a symptom for various illnesses. John's medical records show him ill with "diarrhoea" several times during his service.

The hospital at Strawberry Plains was brand new but its facilities would have included existing buildings. A May 28, 1862, letter from John Goodman, the "sergeon" mentioned above, to Lieutenant John M. Davidson of the 39th North Carolina Volunteer Infantry Regiment details setting up the hospital and hiring staff. Goodman was to be first assistant to principal surgeon Dr. L. Y. Green and was recruiting Davidson for the position of steward and Mrs. Davidson to be matron of the hospital. He estimated they had enough supplies to handle fifty patients as soon as they could get the buildings cleaned, with a proposed census of two hundred patients after more supplies arrived.[5] The hospital was located

---

[3] A good overview of medical treatment during the war, accompanied by photographs, can be found in George W[orthington] Adams, "Caring for the Men," in William C. Davis, ed., *Fighting for Time*, vol. 4 of The Image of War, 1861–1865 (Garden City, NY: Doubleday & Co., 1983), 231–74.

[4] Cunningham, *Doctors in Gray*, 184.

[5] John Goodman to John Mitchell Davidson, letter, May 28, 1862, Davidson Family Papers, housed in Atlanta History Center. A transcript of the letter is in box 2, folder 3 (January–June 1862), and is viewable online in the Davidson Family Papers at www.dlg.galileo.usg.edu.

not far from where the Strawberry Plains post office is today, with ready access to the railroad. More seriously ill patients could be sent on to Knoxville by train. From regimental records we know that at least one of the nurses, farmer William A. Twiggs, had enlisted with John at Morganton. Whether or not he had any medical training is unknown. Twiggs would later figure in a conflict between Union and Confederate sympathizers back home in Fannin County.

Strawberry Plains already had a military presence, Cherokee and highlander troops from the 39th North Carolina Infantry. This was the famous legion founded by William Holland Thomas, the only white man to serve as chief of the Cherokee. The regiment was stationed there to guard the 1600-foot-long bridge owned by the East Tennessee & Virginia Railroad. It had been targeted by Union saboteurs who planned to burn nine bridges from northern Alabama nearly to Virginia in preparation for a Union invasion of the South from Kentucky. In November 1861 an attempt to burn it had been foiled by a lone Rebel soldier, James Keelan (or Keeling), who, despite being shot and stabbed and having one hand cut off, kept the bridge in Rebel control. In Douthit family lore, John was said to have guarded the bridge, but the letters we have indicate that he was ill during much if not all of his time at Strawberry Plains. Still, it is possible that he did some service as a guard before rejoining his regiment. His last letter from there, dated August 21, does not mention being in the hospital.

S. M. Douthit was John's older brother Solomon, born in 1830, who as a schoolteacher received an exemption from military service. Since so many Civil War-era letters do not adhere to letter formulas as strictly as John's did, it is worth asking whether Solomon's teaching curriculum included letter writing from old models and made John value outdated forms. Their brother Andrew (born 1828) was also exempted from service because he was a blacksmith, a crucial occupation for the civilian population.

It is no wonder that John was interested in learning who remained at home. Alfred Weaver, the husband of John's first cousin Margaret and a neighbor on Hot House Creek, was detailed that summer to leave Company H of the 52nd "on detached service arresting deserters."[6] On July 31 Governor Brown issued a proclamation against desertion that was carried in Georgia newspapers. It approved the arrest and jailing of "any officer or soldier absent from his post without leave."[7] In north Georgia, conscription agents were relentless in their efforts to capture those eligible to serve. Confederate troops rounded up both deserters and dissenters from the Southern cause and forced them into the Army. The knowledge that rich people could either hire substitutes or pay hefty bribes to avoid conscription was bitterly resented: "Despite the adamant denials of conscription officers, plain folk viewed them largely as speculators in human flesh attempting to profit, if not monetarily, at least politically.... A bribery attempt could sometimes get one hanged, Not offering a large enough bribe could produce the same result."[8] Jonathan Sarris summarizes the situation for Fannin and surrounding counties:

> Enduring defeat and worrying about problems at home, many north Georgians did desert in 1862 and 1863...at least one quarter of all Fannin [County] men who enlisted in the army deserted at some point in the war....When erstwhile mountain Rebels began to return home in late 1862, they would usually band together in groups and "lay out" in the mountains, concealing themselves from con-

[6] Alfred Weaver, Confederate Service Records, National Archives.
[7] *Southern Federal Union* 33/12 (August 12, 1862): 1.
[8] Williams et al., *Plain Folk in a Rich Man's War*, 111.

scription agents, visiting their homesteads for hurried, se-
cretive reunions with family and friends.[9]

David Williams gives a higher figure, saying that over half
the northeast Georgia troops had deserted by October 1862.[10]
As far as can be determined from his letters, John never considered desertion.

> Hospital No. 2
> Strawberry Plains July 24th 1862
> My Dear Companion I again take my pen in hand to
> let you know how I am getting I can say to you that I am
> mending as fast as could be expected I can go any where
> about the Hospital I have not taken any medicein for three
> or four days I think I am out of danger about eating which
> I don't think will be very hard to do so long as I do not go
> to the table to eat the fare of the Hospital I have no room
> to grumble We have bread and coffee for breakfast Soup
> for dinner and tea for Supper generally I can say to you
> that I received your letter yesterday bearing date July the
> 19th and was exceedingly glad to hear from you and to
> hear that you were in tolerable health it was the first letter
> that I have received since the 30 of June I sent you a letter
> by Mr. Brown which I hope you have received
> [page 2]
> be fore this time I do not know when I will get the chance
> to come home as the doctor here cant give furlows but I
> will come the first opportunity you state that you had
> heard that Yankees had taken Richmond I have never
> heard any such news here nor neither do I ever expect that
> they will be able to take Richmond Since our people have
> gave them such a whipping there I do not know that I
> have any thing more to write tell Julitty her paw wants to
> see her very bad and think that he will come home to see

[9] Sarris, *A Separate Civil War*, 70.
[10] Williams et al., *Plain Folk in a Rich Man's War*, 103.

her I want you to write to every mail and let me know how you are getting along this makes the third letter that I wrote to you since I came to the hospital so nothing more at this time but remains your husband until death

John, M, Douthit
Direct your letters to Strawberry Plains
in care of Sergeon Goodman

Note John's mistrust of hospital food. Intestinal disorders were often attributed to bad food in this era.

The letters preserved by Martha include only one written in the hospital before July 24, not two, as John says, another indication that some letters were lost. She must have been worried to learn he was hospitalized with a fever, for she would have known of neighbors who had died in the same circumstances. By now she was nearing the end of her pregnancy and John was understandably anxious for her as well. It seems from the following letter that she had sent him some details about her health. At least his hospitalization kept him in one place for mail delivery.

Sunday morning
July 27, 1862
Strawberry Plains Tenn
My Dear Companion

I again take my pen in hand to drop you a few lines to let you know that I am still on rising ground I am mending as fast as anyone can be expect to mend though I am still tolerable weak yet I received a letter from you yesterday which was dated the 25th of this month which gave me much satisfaction to hear from you and to hear that you was as well as what you was You also stated that if you did not hear that I was better by Friday that S.M. Douthit and Davis would come to see me I would give almost anything to see them but think they had better not come if

they have not already started when these lines come to
hand I would not recommend them to start as I think I
am out of danger and it will cost them ten or fifteen dollars to come and to go back and would be in danger of
there getting the measles or some other complaint as the
mail is changed you may get this letter and an other the
same mail as the last letter I wrote expected it would get
there on Wednesday You stated that you wished me to try
and come home I wish it was so that I could come home

[page 2]

as I would like to see you and Julitty very much and am
very uneasy about you at this time but there is no chance
for furlow at this time and place as I would have to go to
the Regiment to get a furlow and have it signed up by the
officer of the Regiment and the Brigader general But I
still hope we will live to see better days and the cloud of
war banished a way from our once happy and peaceful
land We have preaching here in hospital every Sunday and
Dr. Goodman has preached for us twice I do not know
what the minister is that is going to preach to day Give
my best respects to inquiring friends So I must come to a
close hoping to hear from you soon So nothing more at
this time but remains your husband until Death

John, M, Douthit

For the first time, John's younger brother Warren Davis
Douthit enters the story. Born in 1840 and married to Harriet
Garren in 1858, Davis, a farmer, should have been in the army
by then. To visit John, the brothers would have taken the same
rail line to Strawberry Plains that took John from Camp
McDonald to Tennessee; there was no other.

A letter from "T.D.W." also discouraged visits to the
troops:

Morristown, August 8, 1862.

Dear Confederacy:…Before I go farther, let me remind all of the friends and relatives of troops here not to imagine that their presence here at this particular junction will benefit them or the cause, besides they will find difficulties innumerable in passing the lines.--I have seen the wives of soldiers arrive here by the cars, some of whom I know, and here they found the only consolation, that conveyance to the camp could not be had--the distance too far to walk, and hardly a house to shelter them if they did go--no hotel here--hardly a spare room to be had for love or money. I have assisted all that I could in procuring conveyance by one single coach--the only one in the county; but I now say to all, that if they do come, they can go no further than 10 miles, and our forces are 18 miles beyond, and still advancing. I mention this not to deter them if they *will* come, but simply to lay before them the difficulty of getting to their destination. Some ladies have come three and four hundred miles and had to return the next day for want of proper accommodations and facilities of transportation…. I conclude with one word more to our friends at home, and that is not to be alarmed--keep cool, do not get excited, fly off at a tangent, but rest quietly, sleep soundly, and trust and hope. Wait for all the facts, and do not believe all the idle rumors you hear. Let me illustrate. A lady came here on the cars today--very much distressed that she could not get to the battle ground, for "she knew Sam was either killed or wounded or something." On inquiry her liege lord was found to be in town and smoking a pipe of high-priced tobacco. T.D.W.[11]

With time on his hands, John wrote to at least one other person during his hospital stay, Martha's sister Julietta Condecy Willson. One wonders whether letters to male friends

---

[11] "T.D.W.," *Southern Confederacy* 2/152 (August 12, 1862): 2.

and relatives would have been more forthcoming about the realities of war. The undated letter to his sister-in-law, written later when he was almost well, is of a piece with those to Martha, neither more nor less informative. Some of the letter was either not photocopied or has been torn away and the original is not available. The missing lines appear to refer to visitors.

> Miss Julitty C. Willson[12]
> Dear Sister,
> It is with pleasure that I take my pen in hand to drop you a few lines, I received a few lines from you yesterday which I read with pleasure, you can not imagine how bad I want to see you and all the friends and especially, Julitty but do not know when I will have the pleasure. I am getting very tired of the Hospital and would not stay here if it was not that two of my company is here sick and I won't leave them until they get able to wait upon themselves, though we fare tolerable here My Regiment is out at the gap or close to it it is thought there will be a fight there before long I think we will soon have, E, Tenn cleaned out. Condecy if I could see you I could tell You more lies in one hour than I can write in a week. You need not expect to hear anything that is reliable from this part of the [lines not photocopied] to us. They visit the hospital every day. Give my best respects to your Father and Mother and write to me as often as you can. Nothing more at this time only remain your Brother, John M. Douthit

In fact, there would be no decisive battle at Cumberland Gap for the duration of the Civil War. The Julitty John refers to in the body of the letter is his daughter, named for her aunt.

John's next letter to Martha is dated three weeks later and responds to the news he had been waiting for.

---

[12] Evidently John took more care when writing to his sister-in-law. Unlike in letters to Martha, he uses appropriate punctuation.

Strawberry Plains August the 21 the, 62 [sic]
My Dear Companion
    I seat my self to drop you a few lines to let you know that I am well at the present time hoping these lines will come to hand and find you well and doing well I received two letters from you yesterday and was glad to hear you had gotten to bear safe. You stated you had another daughter which of course I was glad to hear, though I would much rather it had been a boy. You wanted me to send it a name. I have no name to send it at this time. You can name it to suit your selves and I will be sattisfied. I also received four dollars in one of the letters which was most gladly received. I will come home as soon as I can but do not know when that will be. You must take good care of your self and do not take the hipoe[13] for I am coming home if I live. So I must close nothing more at this time,

John, M, Douthit

Victoria Jane Douthit was born on August 14. For the time being, John was on rising ground, indeed. That same day, August 14, General Edmund Kirby Smith left Knoxville with 12,000 men to invade Kentucky, intending to link up with General Braxton Bragg and his 34,000 troops when that army arrived from Mississippi via Chattanooga.

John was one of the 9,000 troops under Stevenson's command who were left to keep General George Morgan confined at Cumberland Gap.

---

[13] *Hipoe* or *hypo* is a shortening of *hypochondria* and in John's era meant *a morbid depression.*

6

The Kentucky Campaign

By early September John was back on duty. During his hospital stay, he had missed the participation of the 52nd in the Battle of Tazewell, Tennessee, when Rebels engaged Colonel John De Courcy's Federal force, who had ventured away from the Gap on a foraging expedition. Called a skirmish by some, nevertheless it resulted in loss of life on both sides and claimed one member of the 52nd, Thomas R. Nations.[1]

Whether it was because he was out of the hospital and feeling better or because he was relieved of the worry about Baby Victoria's safe arrival, John became more informative in his letters. In the hospital he had gained weight, and on September 4, Colonel Boyd, who had been at home in Georgia recuperating from an illness, returned to command the 52nd. There was good news from Kentucky as well, where on August 30 Kirby Smith had whipped General "Bull" Nelson at Richmond.

With the departure of Smith for Kentucky, Stevenson's division took on the main responsibility for putting pressure on Union forces holding Cumberland Gap.

Camp Near Cumberland Gap

---

[1] In an August 14 letter to his parents, Private William H. Looper of the Georgia 52nd, Company I, described the engagement and listed the participants from his company (Mills Lane, ed., *Dear Mother: Don't grieve about me. If I get killed, I'll only be dead": Letters from Georgia Soldiers in the Civil War* [Savannah, GA: The Beehive Press, 1990], 179).

September 7th 1862

My Dear Companion I take my pen in hand to write you a few lines which will inform you that I am in tolerable health at the present time Hoping these lines will come to hand and find you and the rest of the family well I arrived at this place yesterday after three days travel over the worse road you ever seen All is quiet here this morning and has been ever since I arrived here We are camped within range of the Enemys guns and they could shell us here very easy if they knew where where [sic] we were, they fired over a hundred shots yesterday morning some of which passed overy [sic] the camps and struck the mountain a mile from our camps close to where our cooking is done[2] I do not know how long we will stay here but the next move we make I think we will go to Kentucky and we may have to do some hard fighting be fore we get over the mountain

[page 2]

Marartha [sic] I think you had better sell off all of your sock [stock] that your do not need, and have Some wheat sowed if you can get it done I think it would be best to get some one to take the ground and give you part of the crop have that piece of ground be low the house sowed, that is if Mother is willing for you to have it I do not know when I will get to come home but I think I will get to come between this and cold weather I can say to you that I way more now than I have in four years write to me as soon as this comes to hand and let me know how you are all getting along give my best respects to all inquiring friends specialy to your father and mother so nothing more at the present only remains your husband until death

John, M, Douthit

---

[2] For a discussion of the artillery emplacements at Cumberland Gap and in particular the storied "Long Tom" cannon, see William B. Provine, "The Legend of 'Long Tom' at Cumberland Gap," *Tennessee Historical Quarterly* 24/3 (Fall 1965): 256–64.

Direct your letters to Morristown
Tenn in care of cap
Brown 52 Regt Ga Vol

As the two sides played a waiting game at the Gap, John appears to have had plenty of time to write. No doubt to save paper, he wrote a letter to his sister-in-law on the bottom of the next letter to Martha.

Camp Near Cumberland Gap
Sept the 10th 1862
    My Dear Companion I now take my pen in hand to inform you that I am well at present hoping these will come to hand and find you all well I have no strange news to write you at this time all is quiet here and has been for several days the yanks are holden out on the Gap better than was thought they would, but don't think they can hold out much longer, as some of the prisoners we have taken says they are out of bread but have some bacon and beans yet, you can not imagine how bad I want to see you all I want to come home to see the baby but don't know when I shall get to come Tell my sweet Julity that here paw, will come home to see here as soon as he can The health of the Regment is better than it every has been
[page 2]
I will send you some paper the first chance I have I want you to write to me as often as you can for I would like to hear from you every day if it was posable I will close by subscribing my name Your affectionate husband
John M Douthit

Miss J C, Willson Dear Sister
    I do not know that I have anything to write you at this time more than I would like to see you I can say to you that we have been living high on roasting ears beef flour bread as we have got all the corne for five miles

around that will do to roast and have made a mill mill [sic] out of the bottom of an old canteen so we can do our own grinding as long as we can get corn So nothing more but remains your Brother untill death

John M Douthit

John's feast was General Morgan's famine. Trapped on the high ground while Rebel troops enjoyed the land's bounty and the security of their supply lines, Union troops were starving. On his way north, Kirby Smith had cut their lines of communication, and a clandestine trip to Manchester, fifty miles distant, by two Federals had found no supplies to procure. By September 14, according to Union surgeon B. F. Stevenson, only ten days of half rations remained to feed 12,000 men, not to mention the mules and other animals.[3] The troops of both armies had been in the area for months now, preying on the largely pro-Union farms for food, and Confederate troops sometimes went without as well, despite what John reported. Private Looper's August 14 letter from Tazewell notes, "We have been fed very poorly during the last month; sometimes we have been without food for 3 days at a time."[4] His comment eerily foreshadows the future siege of another "Gibraltar": that of Vicksburg, Mississippi, where the positions of the adversaries would be reversed and John and his companions would be among the besieged and starving.

John's next letter describes what Morgan's troops did to keep their guns, remaining food, and other supplies from falling into Confederate hands when they slipped away in the early hours of September 17 and made their unexpected and daring escape through the punishing terrain of eastern Kentucky, eventually to cross the Ohio River at Greenupsburg

[3] Stevenson, "Cumberland Gap," 15.
[4] Lane, ed., *Dear Mother*, 179.

(now Greenup). Small portions of this letter are damaged by dark patches, making a few words illegible.

Sept the 18th 1862
Camp near Cumberland Gap
My Dear Companion
    I now take my pen in hand to drop you a few lines to let you know that I am well at this time hoping these lines will come to hand and find you all well. I have nothing interesting to write you at present, I think we will leave here in a day or two we keep three days rations cooked and had orders last night to see that they was all ready, and for us to be ready to march by daylight this morning but we are not gone yet 8 ½ [illegible] It is thought the enemy is prearing [sic] to evacuate the Gap they were burning something all night last night, some think they were blowing up there magazines, they was either blowing them up or discharging there cannons very rapidly, I want to see you very bad and would be very glad to hear from you I have not had a letter from you since I left the hospital, I am a feard you do not get the letters I send you Write to me when these lines come to hand mayby it will come to hand some time let me know how you and the children are doing and the [illegible] in general
[page 2]
    Write whether you have sold any of your stock or not and how the stock is doing give my best respects to all inquiring friends So nothing more at this time only remains your affectionate husband until death
John, M, Douthit

The Rebels took possession of the Gap the next day. General George Morgan had held it exactly three months. From Greenupsburg, Kentucky, Morgan wrote in his October 3 report, "On the night of the 17th of September, with the army of Stevenson 3 miles in my front, with Bragg and Marshall on my flanks, and Kirby Smith in my rear, my command marched from Cumberland Gap mid the explosion of mines and magazines and lighted by the blaze of the store-houses of the commissary and quartermaster. The sight was grand. Stevenson was taken completely by surprise."[5] Morgan wrote as if facing south from the Gap, towards Tennessee.

In his next report, written October 12, Morgan remarked on the dilemma he had faced at the Gap, whether to eat the mules or save them to transport the cannons in their escape, for "...without forage the mules must soon perish from hunger and the air become pestilent from their carcasses."[6]

Despite their desire for news from home, soldiers must have dreaded to learn bad news from other parts of the war. A whole generation of friends and relatives were fighting. John probably did not yet know that on September 13, Silas Douthit, who was serving in Virginia with the 60th Georgia Infantry, died of typhoid in Lynchburg's General Hospital No. 1. Silas was John's first cousin and brother of the John Douthit serving in the 39th Georgia.

Meanwhile, General Braxton Bragg, who had assumed command of the Army of Mississippi that summer, was acting on his grand plan to invade neutral Kentucky and install a Confederate governor in Frankfort. George Washington Johnson had briefly served as governor of a shadow Confederate government set up in Russellville in 1861, but he was killed at Shiloh. In fall 1861, General Leonidas Polk had invaded western Kentucky, but General Ulysses S. Grant soon arrived to stymie him. Now, General Humphrey Marshall was poised in western Virginia, General Kirby Smith had bypassed the well-fortified Cumberland Gap and entered the state through Big Creek Gap some thirty miles to the west, and

---

[5] *OR*, ser. 1, vol. 16, pt. 1, p. 991.
[6] *OR*, ser. 1, vol. 16, pt. 1, p. 993.

Bragg was marching from Chattanooga to join up with him. Simon Bolivar Buckner and other Rebel leaders would also be involved, as well as the cavalries of John Hunt Morgan and Joseph Wheeler, all intending to push the Federals back across the Ohio. Traveling with Bragg's army was Richard Hawes, Johnson's Lieutenant Governor, who was to be the new governor of what was hoped would become a Confederate state. Crucial to the plan was the anticipated rush of Kentuckians to join the Rebels. Bragg had 15,000 arms to distribute to the new recruits. On the Union side, General Don Carlos Buell was charged with thwarting them and was slowly maneuvering—too slowly for Lincoln's and General Henry Halleck's tastes—towards a confrontation.

So far, John Douthit felt he had nothing interesting to report to Martha. But now the game was well and truly afoot, and he soon burst into reportage to set down his impressions of the Confederate invasion of Kentucky. In October, back in Tennessee after a grand if punishing adventure, he wrote from Rutledge, a town located on a federal road and the seat of Grainger County. He took such great care with the account that he even used, for the first time, semicolons and parentheses, and he numbered the pages.

Camp Near Rutledge[7]
Tennessee Octo 28th 1862
1st page
Dear Wife
    We are now at Rutledge at the south foot of clinch mountain 33 miles North west of Knoxville at the camps occupied by this Brigade last summer. I propose to give

---

[7] Much of the research on this letter was done by my father, Nolan Fowler, who published the annotated text in an article, "Johnny Reb's Impressions of Kentucky in the Fall of 1862," *The Register of the Kentucky Historical Society* 48/164 (July 1950): 205–15.

you a short history of our march into and out of Kentucky. First I am in Barton's Brigade and in Stevenson's division which consists of Barton, Rains and Taylors Brigades.

On the night of the 17th Sept the Federals burnt and blew up the most of their valuable property in the Gap and when we was roused up at 3 o'Clock A.M. the 18th we had many guesses at the meaning of the fires and explosions and stood under arms till about ten A.M. when we moved for the Gap and reached this strong fortress after a winding march of 5 miles and were well satisfied to find no foe to receive us

Here we lay till 11 o'clock A.M. of the 20th when we marched in pursuit of the retreating foe and marching through volumes of dust with very little and very bad water fourteen miles we slept at the Cumberland ford[8]

Rising with the first peep of day we told off 16 miles through dust with little water which brought us to Goose Creek.[9] Here we failed to cook Rations although we lay till 11 o'clock A.M. of the

(2)[10]

22nd when we turned back and after going five miles took a road leading to Richmond[11] and pushed hard along till midnight when by passing our Battery we caught two hours sleep and then resumed our march over hills and

---

[8] Present-day Pineville, Kentucky.

[9] The Goose Creek community, near Manchester, Kentucky, was the site of the Goose Creek Salt Works. It was located on the Warrior's Path, a trail that George Morgan and his troops used to escape into the mountains of eastern Kentucky. The creek is a tributary of the south fork of the Kentucky River. Although Stevenson abandoned the chase at Goose Creek, George Morgan was bedeviled by John Hunt Morgan and his cavalry as far north as Grayson, in Carter County.

[10] This indicates John's own page numbering. He placed the numbers in an upper corner. I will note them in parentheses.

[11] County seat of Madison County and the site of the Battle of Richmond on August 30, 1862, mentioned above. In 1860, its population was 845.

rocks and at sun up the 23rd we halted to rest having marched 25 miles with but little to eat. Here we run over a guard at an orchard and took a hasty breakfast on apples. After cooking rations we marched at noon and passed on through the little town of London[12] and slept near the town. Our next march brought us to Rock Castle river[13] at the foot of Big hill.[14] The Big hill is 18 miles across and we passed it on the 25th and stoped near a Lime sink which served us with water. Nearly all the water courses are dried from running and standing pools in their beds was our only chance for water and I have frequently seen men getting water out of a pond to cook with and others bathing in it and others watering stock in the same pond.

There is not any water on Big hill save a few springs and they are scarce. Sept. 26 we marched on a pike leading toward Richmond but turning to the left we stoped for the night at Gum spring[15] 14 miles from Lancaster.[16] 27th we passed through some beautiful country the farms surrounded

(3)

by rock stone walls and containing some as fine stock as I ever saw. Plenty was smiling on every hand and our hungry boys did not have much difficulty in getting something to eat. Passing 16 miles we stoped in two miles of Lancaster and slept that night. Resuming the march early 28th

---

[12] County seat of Laurel County. Population in 1860 was 235.

[13] The Rockcastle River, a tributary of the Cumberland River, forms the eastern boundaries of Rockcastle and Pulaski counties and the western boundary of Laurel County.

[14] On August 23, as Kirby Smith's troops moved north, a skirmish took place on Big Hill, south of Richmond in Madison County. Kentucky cavalry units under Col. Leonidas Metcalfe were routed by Louisiana Cavalry with Smith's forces. This was the first engagement of the Kentucky invasion.

[15] A spring near Paint Lick Creek, perhaps named for hollow logs used as bee gums.

[16] County seat of Garrard County. Population in 1860 was 721.

we passed 8 miles pretty country and stoped within two miles of Danville[17] which may be considered the center and chief star of Kentucky—We took up in a walnut and sugar maple grove and though we could not use the sugar tree we made it up by a free use of the walnut. The Black walnut is as common in Kentucky as the oak or hickory is in Georgia. After resting here a day, early the 30th with flying colors and musick to the front we marched into and through town. At this place we met Bragg's troops but made no halt but pressed on and 6 miles brought us to Harrodsburg[18] another pretty town. Along here we received every demonstration of respect from the citizens such as the ladies waving handkerchiefs and small Confederate Flags and giving our ragged boys clothing. Frequently a citizen would feed 50 or a 100 men without price or charge. Along here we suffered much from sore feet which was caused by marching altogether on a firm unyielding Pike road. We stoped for the night near Eldorado[19] on Salt river[20]—

(4)

Apples and sugar cane were plenty along the road and they served to slake our thirst many times when we could not have got water. Orders were very strict against taking any kind of property; but despite of orders I have seen the last hill in a potato patch demolished and the last sugar cane taken from a patch and nearly a half Regiment in an orchard at a time. Orders were very strict against straggling from the Regt. But many nights out of 45 men in our company not more than twelve would stack arms

---

[17] County seat of Boyle County. Population in 1860 was 4,962.

[18] County seat of Mercer County. Population in 1860 was 1,668. Harrodsburg, settled in 1774, is the oldest pioneer settlement in Kentucky.

[19] Today called McAfee, the village is located about six miles north of Harrodsburg. Not listed in the 1860 census.

[20] This river starts in Boyle County and flows north through the middle of Mercer County.

when we would halt. Octo 1st. A early start and hard march passed us through Lawrenceburg[21] and we passed the night two miles from town. 2nd We passed through Rough & Ready[22] and were informed by General Barton that he was expecting to meet the enemy today; So we march 5 miles toward Louisville[23] and finding no foe we turned and came again to Rough & Ready and marched within two miles of Frankfort the Capitol of the state.[24] We were very pleasantly located here and remained here till 4 o'clock P.M. of the 4th day Octo. During the 4th our head men were engaged in making a governor for Kentucky; but he did not warm his seat for we left that evening at quick time.[25] We went through town burnt the car bridge cut the horse bridge and marched on till 3 o'clock A.M. of the 5th across the country to Versailes[26] 14 miles from Frankfort continued—

(5)

continued from 4th page—In going from Frankfort to Versailes our men strggled pretty bad and several of our Regt. and one of our company were taken prisoners by the Federal cavalry. At Versailes I saw thousands of troops and wagons which I had not seen before—in fact the town was full of passing men for hours and I have no idea of the number that passed here on the 5th. Our Brigade stayed

---

[21] County seat of Anderson County. Population in 1860 was 339.

[22] Originally designated by President Zachary Taylor's nickname, today it is the town of Alton. Population in 1870 was 393.

[23] The county seat of Jefferson County and the largest city in the state in 1860, with a population of 68,033.

[24] Also the county seat of Franklin County. Population in 1860 was 3,702.

[25] Generals Bragg and Smith were both present at the ceremony. Richard Hawes was poised to take over as governor when news came that Union forces were advancing on the capitol. Hawes left without assuming office.

[26] The county seat of Woodford County. Population in 1860 was 1,142. It was the headquarters of Kirby Smith's Army of Kentucky.

here till 2 o'clock P.M. of the 8th.[27] We got as good water here as there is in Kentucky and were happy of the privilege of resting.[28] The citizens though not strongly southern treated us with great kindness and we had no trouble in getting anything the country afforded to eat. In this place I will say we did not suffer but very little for rations on our march into Kentucky; but what we suffered on our retreat the sequel will show.

Leaving Versailes 2 o'clock P.M on the 8th 10 miles brought us near Lawrenceburg where we lay over till 3 o'clock A.M. 9th At 11 o'clock P.M. on the 8th the enemy left Lawrenceburg and early the 9th we entered and secured over a hundred prisoners of the sick and stragglers—Our cavalry had a sharp little fight about a mile off with the enemies pickets and sent in several prisoners—.[29] We stood under arms till sun up and marched and counter

---

[27] The Battle of Perryville, the largest battle on Kentucky soil, took place on October 8. The 41st Georgia fought in the 3rd, or Maney's Brigade, in General B. F. Cheatham's Division. The division comprised General Leonidas Polk's right wing, numbering some 7,000 men. Brigadier George Early Maney (1826–1901) was a Tennessee lawyer and legislator who had fought in the Mexican War. Other regiments of the future Barton's Brigade did not participate.

[28] Kentucky was in the grip of a drought from mid-August to late October.

[29] Brigadier General Joshua W. Sill, US Army, reported to General Buell on October 9, "Left Frankfort 1 a.m. yesterday. By arriving at Lawrenceburg the rebel cavalry appeared in front and a sharp skirmish ensued, owing to the imprudent advance of Jacob's cavalry. The leading company lost 3 killed, 12 wounded, 13 missing. Several of the enemy killed and wounded, I doubt not. Our march from Lawrenceburg was closely watched by the enemy's cavalry, and at daybreak of to-day they appeared in force and attempted to drive in the pickets. They exhibited three regiments of infantry and one of cavalry. Our pickets were re-enforced and a sharp firing was kept up for three or four hours.... The enemy must have suffered very severely. Many of their men were seen to fall. I presume they picked up some of our stragglers..." (OR, ser. 1, vol. 16, pt. 1, p. 1134).

(6)

marched along the road to Eldorado while Withers Division[30] was engaged to our right near ten miles off. The heavy booming of artillery greeted our ears nearly all day The frightened citizens were leaving their homes all along the road not knowing when or where the fury of battle might rage. Our folks captured 600 prisoners and a train of 58 wagons loaded with commissary stores. On the 8th a cavalry [engagement] took place on the ground we passed today and left some dead horses and other evidence of man's fallen depraved nature. On the night of the 9th we stoped to rest and sleep near Eldorado on the ground occupied by us on the night of the 30th Sept. An early start and hard march took us to Harrodsburg and passing through town the citizens and our cavalry informed us that the enemy were only three miles off and advancing. We marched out meeting them and took up position for battle and unpacked knapsacks ready to do or die for Liberty. Our position was two miles south west of Town. Our signal corps were busy waving their flags on the right and left of our line and some of men said they saw the enemies cavalry half a mile off.

(7)

We had about ten thousand men in line in my sight (our division is that strong) and were under strict orders to keep in our places and ready; but in five minutes the boys were out cracking walnuts and getting corn and punkins for supper and starting an occasional Rabbit the men would join in the shout as though no enemy was near Our cavalry passed to the front and we stacked arms and began to prepare for the night. An east wind blew up a very cool rain and having nothing better we made use of a string of

---

[30] Major General Jones Mitchell Withers (1814–1890) of Alabama, veteran of the Mexican War, lawyer, merchant, mayor of Mobile, and state legislator. He was not at Perryville, General Bragg having ordered his division to move towards Frankfort.

fence near by. Shivering and wet we passed the night away
and were glad to be ordered into line before day and on
the march. We double quicked a good deal on the 10th
and marching rapidly were passed by general Bragg about
noon who had us stopped and put a slower gait. We
guarded a cross road 3 hours till our wagon trains got out
of danger on the road to Camp Breckinridge;[31] and then
we left the main road and traveled over some rough country down to Dick's River[32] and crossing we went up a Very
steep hill (at whose foot we saw blood and a bier stained
with blood) and moving on a mile we camped with the

(8)

main army whose camp fires illuminated the whole country round for miles. Here being bravely lead on by a captain and 2 or 3 Lieutenants we fearlessly attacked a hen
roost and company H not being slow got her full share of
the poultry. Hearing our wagons were captured we went
to sleep without supper save parch corn and our chickens;
but our wagons rolled up about midnight and a cooking
detail had us a good breakfast for the 11th day of Octo.
Remaining here till sunset of the 13th we cooked 4 days
rations while the main army were getting in motion. In
preparing our Rations we failed to cook a part and wasted
a part and were then informed we must do on what we got
8 days. Starting at sunset we passed through Bryantsville[33]
and on to Camp Breckinridge where we got just what

---

[31] General Bragg briefly established Camp Breckinridge some seven
miles north of Lancaster at Hoskins Crossroads at the site of the Union
recruiting station Camp Dick Robinson, as a training camp for Confederate troops. Following Perryville and the subsequent retreat of Confederate
forces, the camp returned to Union hands and was renamed Camp Nelson
in honor of General William "Bull" Nelson.
[32] Today's Dix River. A tributary of the Kentucky River which joins it
near High Bridge, KY.
[33] About nine miles north of Lancaster, in Garrard County. No population figures for 1860.

Pickle pork we could carry and left a great deal which was destroyed and passing on we got in a mile of Lancaster[34] about midnight where being halted regardless of the cool air we fell down by the road side and slept till our wagon trains got ahead then rousing up and jogging on we passed through town and halted not far from town while some government property was burning in town—to be continued

(9)

Here we lay till about ten o'clock A.M. of the 14th and here we heard the roaring of cannon that was playing near town furiously while Rains Brigade and Morgans Cavalry[35] engaged the enemy beyond town. We then moved on a short distance and took up in line of Battle an hour by sun and lay till ten o'clock P.M. when we were ordered to march in silence. Rousing up at that hour we rushed on at a quick pace for three or four miles and overtook the main army about six miles from town; Here we fell down by the road side about midnight and notwithstanding the cool air we slept and nodded for two hours until the main army moved out of the way and then we pushed on until sunrise when being fourteen miles from town we were ordered to rest. The first time the order was given us since the 13th this being the 15th. We move a short distance and took up where we remained till late of the evening of the 16th. Here we had nothing to eat but parched corn; Moving on about eight miles

(10) we slept near the foot of Big hill till about day when we started up it and pressed on till late at night and

---

[34] The army split here. Bragg took the more direct route to Cumberland Gap through Crab Orchard, Mt. Vernon, and London. Smith and his troops, with Stevenson's division bringing up the rear, took a more indirect route to reach the Gap. This sped up the retreat and made pursuit more difficult.

[35] Col. John Hunt Morgan (1825–1864), leader of the legendary cavalry unit Morgan's Raiders.

having gone eighteen or twenty miles we halted at Rock Castle river for the night. At midnight our wagons came to us (they had been ahead) and we cooked a little bread for two days rations.[36] 18th. At day light we moved on and going our usual distance of 18 miles we stoped for the night having left the road we came into Kentucky about two miles from the river. From here on to the gap hog skins and chicken feathers were plenty showing that hungry men had gone ahead of us and from here on our suffering increased until we got to the Gap on the 23rd day of October.

We came out of Kentucky before the enemy but they feared us and did not press us any—We burnt up and destroyed a good deal of property but we took it all from the Yankees. Nearly all our wagons have been taken

(11)

from our foes—we brought out a great many horses mules wagons Beeves and commissary stores. We marched about 450 miles in thirty three days and passing the gap the 23rd we continued on marching and passing through Knoxville we are now located About ten miles above Loudon near the Station of Lanore.[37]

I received your letter of the 6th of last month and glad to hear from you as it was the first that I had heard from you since August. I want you to write to me as soon as these lines come to hand direct your letters to Knoxville I do not now how long we will stay here nor where we will go when we leave here some thinks we will go down to-

---

[36] On October 17, General Kirby Smith sent a dispatch to General Leonidas Polk from the Rockcastle River, reporting that General Stevenson "has just arrived on the opposite side of the river, having marched 30 miles since last evening, besides aiding their artillery and ordnance grain up the Big Hill" (*OR*, ser. 1, vol. 16, pt. 2, p. 960).

[37] The estate of General William Lenoir (1751–1839), who had fought at Kings Mountain and had been deeded 5,000 acres for his service during the Revolution.

wards Nashville but I do not know where give my best respects to all inquiring friends nothing more at present

John. M. Douthit

On October 22, General Kirby Smith wrote to Bragg
from Cumberland Gap, "General: The head of my command
has just arrived here. My men have suffered on this march
everything excepting actual starvation. There must be not less
than 10,000 of them scattered through the country trying to
find something upon which to live."[38]

On October 26 at Rutledge, Captain Augustus F. "Gus"
Boyd of the 52nd, company B, wrote a shorter summary of the
invasion and retreat for his sister. Of John's "very cool wind"
on the 9th, Boyd said, "Soon night came on and a terrible
night it was. For it rained fast and froze. Every thing was covered with sleet...."[39] Boyd specified that the troops did not
know they were retreating back to Tennessee until they got to
Camp Dick "Robberson." "I cannot give any more particulars,"
Boyd says in his next paragraph, "for I am so cold that I can
hardly hold my pen....the snow is falling fast."[40]

Conditions had deteriorated steadily during the withdrawal. The weather turned and it began to snow. Marching
with the 1st Tennessee under Bragg's command, Sam Watkins remembered bitterly twenty years later, "From Perryville
we went to Camp Dick Robinson and drew three days' rations, and then set fire to and destroyed all those great depos-
its of army stores which would have supplied the South for a
year. We ate those rations and commenced our retreat out of
Kentucky with empty haversacks and still emptier stomachs."[41]

---

[38] *OR*, ser. 1, pt. 1, vol. 16, p. 970.
[39] Lane, ed., *Dear Mother*, 195.
[40] Lane, ed., *Dear Mother*, 195.
[41] Watkins, *Co. Aytch*, 51.

Virge Moose of the Georgia 52nd, Company C, also remembered the odd feast-and-famine destiny of the food acquired at Camp Dick Robinson and what happened to it on the march:

> We expected a great battle on the following day, but some time in the night we were ordered to silently steal away, and we went by a place called Dick Robinson, where the whole neighborhood was covered with pickel pork, four or five feet deep, that we had boried from the yankees and never intended to pay back.
>
> Our officers told us to take what we wanted as we marched through and we would stick our bayonet through about twenty-five pounds and shoulder our guns with the pork and we looked just like an army of giants with white hats on. After we all got what we wanted the rest was set on fire and we left by the light of it.
>
> Pretty soon you would see a fellow take his knife and cut his piece in two and throw half of it down, as it was too heavy to carry. I think they all did. I know I did, and the sides of the road were literally covered with meat. But it was not many days until we wished that we had not been so extravagant....We were nearing Cumberlin Gap....I had not ate a single mouthful for four days, neither had I slept any in that length of time.[42]

The soldiers kept expecting to be given rations, but they walked mile after mile, hour after hour, night and day, with little or nothing. Sam Watkins wrote that they were so desperate that, coming upon a wild heifer, "We killed and skinned her; and I cut off about five pounds of hindquarter: In

---

[42] Virge Moose [Frederick V. Moose], *War Reminisces: A Collection of War Stories as Remembered by Virge Moose, Company C, 52nd Georgia Infantry Regiment, Army of Tennessee—Confederate States of America*, "as they appeared in the *Dahlonega Signal*, 1891." Compiled with preface by Cynthia Adair Coan, undated photocopy in soft cover, p. 34.

three minutes there was no sign of that beef left to tell the tale. We ate that beef raw and without salt."[43]

Since Barton's Brigade was part of the division protecting the rear of the army, they might have been following a plague of locusts for all the food they could find on the march back to Tennessee. Also, they were bedeviled by the pursuing enemy. Morgan's cavalry was with them only until October 17, when Morgan decided to fight in Kentucky rather than retreat and took his men back northward. When the ragged, worn-out troops reached Rutledge, some without shoes, warm clothing, or tents, they camped in four inches of snow.

One soldier of particular interest to John did not survive the retreat. Probably John did not even know that his first cousin John Douthit, now a second sergeant with the 39th Georgia Company I and brother of Silas Douthit (who himself had died in September), died as the retreating troops crossed the Cumberland River on October 18, leaving a young wife at home.

As usual, John downplays both the seriousness of his situation and his part in reported events. Payroll records show that on or about October 16, John was promoted from private to second sergeant. According to Hardee's manual, the second sergeant acts as a "file closer" and "In manoeuvres he will be designated the left guide of the company."[44]

Discussions continue about the wisdom of Bragg's withdrawal from Kentucky after Perryville. Outnumbered three to one and without either sufficient supplies or significant support from Kentucky citizens, Bragg felt he had to preserve his

---

[43] Watkins, *Co. Aytch*, 52.

[44] William Joseph Hardee, *Rifle and Light Infantry Tactics: for the exercise and manoevres of troops when acting as light infantry or riflemen/prepared under the direction of the War Department* (Nashville, TN: J.O. Griffith, 1861), 7.

army to fight another day. In a speech at Camp Dick Robinson (renamed Camp Breckinridge by the Confederates) delivered the day before he gave the order to withdraw, he explained,

> Buell is massed on our right and closes access to Nashville. We whipped him at Perryville, but another such a victory will be fatal to us. He is near his supplies and reinforcements; we are distant from ours. Kentucky won't come to our relief. Wallace is in our rear, with the great North fully roused and at his back. If we attempt to reach Virginia through the mountain passes of Eastern Kentucky, we will starve. We are in a jug and with but a simple outlet, and that is through Cumberland Gap. We must take that route and take it now, or the last man of us all will be captured.[45]

On the Union side, Buell's decision not to pursue the retreating Confederates past London generated an investigation by his superiors. Major General Lewis Wallace, president of the commission that investigated Buell, concluded,

> The evidence establishes that General Buell received information on the night of the 11th that Bragg had crossed the river to Camp Dick Robinson; yet he made no determined movement with the main body of his army until 12 o'clock the night of the 13th. From the morning of the 9th to the night of the 11th he waited to learn whether his enemy would cross the river.... Finally, on the night of the 13th...he started Crittenden's corps through Danville toward Crab Orchard. It was then too late; Bragg with his column and all his train had passed the point of interception. To this delay we are compelled to attribute the escape of the rebels from Kentucky.[46]

---

[45] Quoted in Stevenson, "Cumberland Gap," 7.
[46] *OR*, ser. 1, vol. 14, pt. 1, p. 12.

Buell's choice not to follow was partly based on the impossibility of feeding his army and acquiring drinking water from what they could find in the wake of the departing Rebels. For this reluctance to strike a definitive blow, he was soon replaced by William Rosecrans.

So the Georgia troops were back where they started, some forty miles south of the Gap. The expected influx of recruits from the Kentucky countryside had not materialized. Mistakes and indecision kept the Confederates from following up on Kirby Smith's promising beginning. They had also been outnumbered. Bragg's grand design had come to naught, and the sovereignty of Kentucky would never again be threatened. A newspaper reporter accompanying the Confederate troops filed this report dated October 24, 1862:

> The combined armies of General Bragg and Kirby Smith, including the forces of McCown, Stephenson [sic], and Marshall, began their retrograde movement on the thirteen instant, from Dick's River, not far distant from Harrodsburg, Ky., General Bragg's force leading and passing out of the State ahead of General Smith. Many of the men are worn out with almost constant marching, by day and night, pinched a great portion of the time by hunger and thirst, and having to subsist a good portion of the time on parched corn, pumpkins, etc., and drinking frequently water from holes. How different the feelings of officers and men of these armies now, compared with what they were upon their entrance into Kentucky two months since! It is unnecessary for me to say that the expedition of the confederate forces into Kentucky, has resulted in a miserable failure.[47]

---

[47] *Columbia Sun*, quoted in Frank Moore, ed., *The Rebellion Record* (New York: G.P. Putnam & Sons, 1863), vol. 6.

On October 9, as the retreat after Perryville was getting underway, Major General John C. Pemberton and his family arrived in Mississippi to begin his command over Mississippi and the part of Louisiana east of the Mississippi River.[48] This appointment would foretell the future of John and his fellow soldiers.

[48] Michael C. Ballard, *Pemberton: The General Who Lost Vicksburg* (Jackson, MS: University Press of Mississippi, 1999), 114.

7

Middle Tennessee

Several changes took place in and around the Georgia regiments while they recuperated and waited for action, camped along the Tennessee River near Lenoir's Station. Colonel Boyd, commander of the 52nd, had fallen ill again and was hospitalized in Macon, Georgia. There a Doctor William Doughty pronounced him unfit for service. "Nothing but an abiding conviction of my total physical inability to discharge the duties of the office could induce me to resign," wrote Boyd in his November 1 resignation letter to Inspector General Cooper in Richmond. "But great exposure and fatiguing Marches in the Spring season brought on me a severe spell of fever accompanied with Diarrhea (which last disease remains) & reduced me to a mere Skeleton—and now I have neither flesh nor strength, scarcely sufficient to walk. I fear I am wrecked for life."[1] Boyd would live until 1893. Captain Charles D. Phillips was named as his replacement and promoted to colonel. Major James J. Findley, also of the 52nd, resigned on November 20 and returned to north Georgia, where he joined the Georgia militia. Boyd's seventeen-year-old son Gus was made a captain in Company B of the 52nd.

---

[1] Wier Boyd, handwritten letter, 1 November 1862, Confederate Service Records, National Archives.

Meanwhile, in middle Tennessee, General Bragg was massing troops south of Nashville, near Murfreesboro. Called to Richmond to defend his actions in the failed invasion of Kentucky and to respond to the criticisms lodged by his subordinates, Bragg had come away from the meeting with Jefferson Davis's continued support. But his subordinates were left in place as well, so bad feelings persisted. For the time being, General Buell was defending Nashville and Bragg needed more troops.

November 11, 1862
Camp Near Lenoir's Station Tenn
Dear Companion
I now take my pen in hand to write you a few lines which leaves me in common health at this time hoping when these lines come to hand they will find you all well and doing well I have nothing new nor interesting to write you at this time I think we will move from here in a day or two but do not know for certain where we will go some says that we are ordered ten miles below Loudon on the rails road others think that we will go from here to Kingston Tenn and from there to Murfursborough or between there and Nashville but I do not know which place we will go whether either or not I think we will draw our money today or to morrow if we do I will send it home the first chance I have I think I will get to come home some time between this and spring I think when we take winter quarters
[page 2]
they will forlow [furlough] all home that has not been at home You need not make me any clothes now as I have two suits of those that I brought from home with me and I drawed one over coat which will be as many as I can carry So I will close give my love to your father and mother and tell Condecy to write to me I had half quire of paper that I intended to have sent you but I lost it in Kentucky

and have not had any chance to get any since we have gotten back in to Tennessee Nothing more at this time only
remains your husband until death

John, M, Douthit
direct your letters to Knoxville

Martha must have told John she was having trouble finding paper. The South was experiencing many shortages and
interruptions of services. John was not the only one with mail
troubles. From Rutledge, his brigade commander Brigadier
General Seth M. Barton wrote his family that he had not
heard from them since July.[2]

November 12, 1862
Camped near Lenoirs Station Tenn
 Dear Wife You will find forty dollars enclosed which
I send you we drawed for five months and twenty-seven
days I would send you more but we may not draw any
more for five or six months you can use the money as you
think best I started you a letter yesterday by mail You may
get this before you receive that You kneed not send me
any clothes without it is a pair of socks and my gloves
though if you have me a wooling shirt and drawers you
may send them I may need them after while and have no
chance to get them Write soon and often I am well at the
present We have rations cooked ready to march I think we
will leave here in the morning but do not know where we
will go So good bye for the present

---

 [2] Quoted in Goodson, "Part II—Letters and Diaries," *Georgia Confederate 7,000*, 37.

[page 2]

I will send the money by I A Vanzant[3] and not put it in the letter While I was writing I supposed there was to be a man detailed to go home and bring the company clothes which I suppose is not the case and consequently you will have no chance to send me any clothes though I need nothing but my gloves

John M. Douthit

The monthly pay for a private in the Confederate army was eleven dollars. Pay for sergeants began at seventeen dollars per month. Using the Consumer Price Index inflation calculator as a basis for multiplication, eleven dollars comes to $261.39 in today's money. The forty dollars John sent home would thus be equivalent to $950.52 today. Confederate money would eventually be worthless, but not in 1862. Rebel soldiers were not paid as frequently as Union soldiers were, hence the several weeks' pay John received.

The November 12 letter was the last one John sent from east of the Cumberland Mountains. In mid-November a corps in eastern Tennessee was sent to join Bragg's Army of Tennessee (formed from his reorganized Army of Mississippi) in central Tennessee. Most of the troops relocated by rail. But their supplies traveled by wagon train, and Georgia troops, including the 52nd, were detailed to march overland and guard them. A diary kept by Captain Rufus R. Asbury of the 52nd places the regiment seven miles from Kingston, Tennes-

---

[3] Lieutenant Isaac Avery Vanzant, a graduate of the University of Georgia Medical School in Augusta. He would be captured at Missionary Ridge and imprisoned at Johnson's Island. Like the Douthits and the Willsons, the Vanzants had been among the first white settlers in the Fannin County area and like them had neighbored with the Cherokee before the removal. Vanzant's rural store and post office was a well-known gathering place in Fannin County.

see, on November 16. From there they marched "down the ravine" to Chattanooga and up Walden Ridge, which runs along the eastern edge of the Cumberland Plateau. It rained hard the nineteenth, when they camped "upon top of the mountain." They then crossed the ridge, descended into the Sequatchie Valley, marching sixteen to eighteen miles a day, and camped at Jasper, Tennessee on the twenty-third. In the next two days they covered thirty-five miles and passed Sewanee, where the University of the South was under construction. The cornerstone had been consecrated in 1860 by Episcopalian bishop Leonidas Polk, a wealthy slaveholder in Maury County, Tennessee, who would come to be known in the war as "the fighting bishop." On Wednesday, November 26, another eighteen miles brought them to their destination, "near Manchester on the McMinnville Rail Road."[4]

Middle Tennessee was more sympathetic to the Confederate cause than the eastern part of the state, perhaps making life a little easier for the Rebels. Yet a plaintive note creeps into John's letters. He had been gone from home eight months and had seen enough illness, death, and privation to last a lifetime; but he had not set eyes on his now three-month-old baby daughter. The war ground on, with the fading promise of a furlough dancing about like a will-o-the-wisp. As to the future, as usual there was nothing to rely on but camp rumors.

November the 27th 1862
Manchester, Tenn[5]
Dear Wife

---

[4] Diary of Captain Rufus R. Asbury, transcribed by Scott Le Craw, General Barton & Stovall History/Heritage Association, online newsletter, December 2015. He refers to the McMinnville & Manchester Railroad.

[5] A town in Coffee County, Tennessee, located on the Little Duck River. Population in 1860 was 315.

I write you again to let you know that I am still alive and well at the present time. We reached this place yesterday evening. Manchester is a small place on the railroad. The cars do not run here now. We marched eleven days out of thirteen that we were on the road. We are now thirty miles from Murfreesburrow[6] and sixty from Nashville.[7] Some think there will be a fight here though the enemy is fifty miles off. I have not time to give you a full account of our march to this place. How long we will stay here I can not tell you. I want you to write as often as you can I want to hear from you very bad at this time. Direct your letters Knoxville. Ive nothing more at this time so only remains your husband until death

John, M, Douthit

Situated at the foot of the Cumberland Plateau on I-24 southwest of Nashville, today Manchester is known for the George Dickel Distillery and the Bonnaroo Music Festival. In the Civil War era it produced textiles and railroad crossties. John's time there was taken up with drilling and with trying to stay warm and dry, which was impossible due to the scarcity of tents, the frequent rain, and frigid weather.

Although the 52nd had not fought in a major engagement, its numbers continued to dwindle. Illness and fatalities in skirmishes had taken some. Others had been captured in the retreat from Kentucky. The devastation of Perryville was on everyone's minds. Desertions increased. By now John must have been thinking that he could not take survival for granted.

From his headquarters in Tullahoma, General Bragg described the larger picture in General Order 151, dated No-

---

[6] Murfreesboro, county seat of Rutherford County. Population in 1860 was 466.

[7] County seat of Davidson County as well as the state capital, located on the Cumberland River. Population in 1860 was 16,988.

vember 20. The Army of Tennessee comprised three corps named after their commanders: (Kirby) Smith's, (Leonidas) Polk's, and (William J.) Hardee's. They were to be joined by the cavalry brigades of John Hunt Morgan and Nathan Bedford Forrest. Polk's corps was deployed near Murfreesboro, Smith's near Manchester, and Hardee's near Shelbyville. Bragg declared, "The foregoing dispositions are in anticipation of the great struggle which must soon settle the question of supremacy in Middle Tennessee. The enemy in heavy force is before us, with a determination, no doubt, to redeem the fruitful country we have wrested from him. With the remembrance of Richmond, Munfordville, and Perryville so fresh in our minds, let us make a name for the now Army of Tennessee as enviable as those enjoyed by the armies of Kentucky and the Mississippi."[8] In the report he included Kirby Smith's numbers for the Department of East Tennessee. Smith's first division, commanded by Carter L. Stevenson, was made up of three brigades. The First Brigade, led by Seth M. Barton, comprised the 30th and 31st Alabama, the 40th and 52nd Georgia, the 9th Georgia Battalion, and the Botetourt (Virginia) Artillery. Rains and Taylor commanded the other two brigades. With 119 officers and 2,131 enlisted men, Barton's Brigade totaled 3,020 men present and 1,393 others on the rolls but absent for whatever reason. The entire division totaled 9,133 men with another 3,999 not present. Stevenson had occupied the Gap, had led the pursuit of George Morgan into Kentucky, and had captured the Union garrison at Munfordville. As a result of his successes, he had been promoted to major general in October of that year.

---

[8] *OR*, ser. 1, vol. 20, pt. 2, pp. 411–12.

December the 4th 1862
Manchester Tenn
Dear Companion

I write you again to let you know that I am well at the present time hoping these few lines will come to hand and find you all well I have nothing special or interesting to write you at this time onley I am very anxious to hear from you We are still at Manchester and have cleaned off our camps as though we was going to stay here some time but do not know how long we will stay here We may stay here until spring but we never know one day what we will do the next it is my opinion that we will stay here a month or two and probably all winter perhaps you would like to know how we have to fare as for provisions we have plenty that is of beef flour bacon and corn meal as for shelters or tents we have but two for the company and have to take the weather as it comes though the weather has been very favorable until sum time since I think we will get tents before long as the weather is getting two cold for men to stand it like cattle I do not know what number of soldiers there is at this place now the papers will give you a better idea for the number than I can

[page 2]

Every thing is fine here and some of the boys has made money speculating on apples while others have spent nearly all they have I will give you prises of a few articles apples is worth from fifty cents to one dollar per dozen tobacco one dollar a plug milk fifty cents a quart pork twenty five cents per pound bacon forty cents and all other articles in proportion if you make any corn you will do well to take special care of it for bread will be scarce be fore corn is made again when you write to me again write how every thing is doing and how you are getting along about salt If you have any chance I want you to send me my over coat and some socks I sold the over coat that we drawed while on the march to this place it was two heavy to carry Give

my best respects to your father and mother So nothing
more but remain your affectionate husband until death

John M. Douthit

Write soon direct your letter to Chattanooga Tenn

Due to the blockades squeezing commerce as well as une-
qual distribution of goods, salt was one of the most direly
needed commodities in the South, necessary for curing meat
above all. Georgia established salt lists to distribute what could
be secured, and soldiers' families were given priority. The
overcoat was needed now as there was little shelter and it
snowed again in early December. The corps moved fourteen
miles east to Readyville, where a gristmill was located on the
Stones River. The Readyville Mill has been restored and is in
operation today. John says "Readersville," but this is an error.
From "Reeders Vill TN" Private Robinson reported, "...it
Snowed on Saturday & we had to Start on Sunday nite we was
marcht out on the Side of a hill to camp whare the Snow was
ankle deep we Raket away the Snow & Burnt fence Rails &
we though Rested well the next day the Road about 12 was
about ankle deep in mud...." He added that the troops hadn't
had any salt "cence away long last month...."[9]

Readersville Tenn
December the 12 1862
Dear Companion
    I write you again to let you know that I am well and
hope these few lines will come to hand and find you all
well I have nothing of importance to write you at this time
I received your letter of November the 16th and was glad
to hear from you and to hear that you was well we left
Manchester the 7 we were two days marching from there
to this place we are now ten or twelve miles from Mur-

---

[9] Robinson, letter, December 9, 1862.

fursbborough I do not know how long we will be here not very long I don't expect I think there will be a general fight some where between here and Nashville some time this winter I understand that Morgan taken twenty two hundred prisoners a day or two ago There has several of the boys of this company deserted and gone home I want to come home and see you all but if I never get to come until I desert I don't think I will ever come Though I think I will get to come home sometime between this and spring Some thinks the war will have to close for the want of provisions though I think there will be provisions enough

[page 2]

To last us twelve months longer I have marched since the 20th of September nearly one thousand miles You must do the best you can until I come home if I ever do I still hope I will see this war ended and to live at home again give my compliments to all of my friends Write to me every week whether you get a letter from me or not Tell Condecy if I could see her I could tell her something about hard times hard marching etc. So I will close for the present So nothing more at present but remains your husband until death

John M Douthit

If General Bragg had anything to say about it, neither John nor anyone else would be going home. After Shiloh, Bragg complained, "Universal suffrage, furloughs, and whiskey have ruined us."[10] By universal suffrage, he meant the practice of letting troops elect their officers. He wanted men in camp, not elsewhere for any reason. When deserters were caught, he had them shot. The number of desertions fell, but still men went home. After Bragg was replaced by Joseph E. Johnston

---

[10] Robert Debs Heinl, Jr., *The Dictionary of Military and Naval Quotations* (Annapolis, MD: Naval Institute Press, 1966), 196.

later in the war, Sam Watkins noted approvingly, "[Johnston] allowed us what General Bragg had never allowed mortal man—a furlough."[11]

John's remark about Morgan surely refers to John Hunt Morgan and his raiders capturing a garrison of Union troops at Hartsville on December 7, much to the alarm of President Lincoln. The next week, Jefferson Davis himself visited Murfreesboro to review a company of the Army of Tennessee as part of a longer trip (December 10, 1862–January 5, 1863) through his western dominions to rally citizens to the cause. He found the company he reviewed to be in excellent condition. In Murfreesboro he promoted John Hunt Morgan to Brigadier General and attended a gala for the dashing thirty-seven-year-old cavalryman and his intended bride, twenty-two-year-old Martha Ready,[12] before moving on. On December 14, while John and his fellow soldiers were shivering around fires in the snow, Morgan and Martha married in Murfreesboro. The ceremony, attended by a number of Confederate officers, including Generals Bragg, Cheatham, and Hardee as well as John C. Breckinridge, former vice president of the US, was officiated by Lieutenant General Leonidas Polk, second cousin of President James K. Polk. Bishop Polk wore his churchly vestments over his military uniform.

While in Murfreesboro, Davis did something else that would determine the fate of John and his comrades: he ordered Carter Stevenson's division transferred to Vicksburg to augment General John C. Pemberton's forces. This directive ran counter to the wishes of General Bragg as well as those of General Joseph E. Johnston, who had just been given com-

---

[11] Watkins, *Co. Aytch*, 111.

[12] Martha "Mattie" Ready (1840–1887) was the daughter of attorney and Tennessee congressman Charles Ready (1802–1878). Their family founded Readyville.

mand of the area stretching from western North Carolina to Mississippi and Louisiana. But, Davis reasoned, Vicksburg and the control of the Mississippi were bigger prizes than central Tennessee.

On December 19, the Georgia 52nd and their fellow regiments under the command of Stevenson marched to Murfreesboro and camped for the night. On the twentieth they traveled by train to Chattanooga. The lack of uniform track width necessitated frequent changes from there on. Over the next several days, the troops took another train to Atlanta, changed for West Point, Georgia, then changed trains yet again to travel to Montgomery, Alabama. They proceeded to Paul's Landing, from whence they went by steamboat to Mobile. In Mobile, they caught another train for Mississippi and eventually arrived at Jackson. They marched to Vicksburg, where on December 28 they arrived directly into what would come to be known as the Battle of Chickasaw Bayou.[13]

---

[13] Asbury diary, December 19–28, 1862, unpaged.

8

Chickasaw Bayou

On December 19, the same day that John and his fellow
Georgians began their journey to relieve Vicksburg, Jefferson
Davis toured the fortifications of the city with General Joseph
E. Johnston. The "Gibraltar of the West," situated on a bluff
above the Mississippi River, shared features with another Gibraltar, Cumberland Gap. It, too, commanded a high defensive position; and like the Gap, it could be isolated and besieged. President Lincoln was determined to seize the city. As
a young man, he had worked on riverboats going to New Orleans and he understood Vicksburg's strategic importance,
which he judged to be even greater than that of New Orleans.
In oft-quoted remarks, Lincoln called Vicksburg the key to
victory and concluded, "The war can never be brought to a
close until that key is in our pocket." Secure Vicksburg and the
Mississippi, and the Confederacy would be cut in two and
would lose the biggest supply line in the country.

In May of that year, Major-General Martin Luther
Smith, a West Point-trained engineer, had designed and built
defenses for Vicksburg. In the fall, Major Samuel Henry
Lockett, another West Pointer, who was chief engineer of the
Department of Mississippi and Louisiana, supervised the construction of more fortifications. President Davis was satisfied
with what he saw: forts, rifle pits, trenches, breastworks,
redans, redoubts, and lunettes, spread in a 6.5-mile cordon

over cliffs and ravines difficult to assail. There were also some twenty-five miles of bluffs to guard, stretching up the river from Vicksburg: Chickasaw Bluffs, also called Walnut Hills. At this time, General Pemberton had only 6,000 men on duty and begged his superiors for reinforcements. Most of his troops had been sent miles to the north to counter Grant's advance. In Arkansas, General Theophilus Holmes kept finding reasons not to send any of the 50,000 men under his command to the aid of Vicksburg.

Also on December 19, General William Tecumseh Sherman and Admiral David Porter left Memphis at the head of a Union naval fleet carrying some 30,000 men down the Mississippi River. Sherman would take on more troops at Helena, Arkansas. It was his first independent field command. Grant, leading the other 40,000 troops of the Army of the Tennessee, intended to bring his forces to Vicksburg overland and draw the troops defending Vicksburg outside the city while Sherman's troops, with protection from Porter's navy, would take it.

But the next day, when John Douthit was boarding a train in Murfreesboro, Grant's enormous supply depot at Holly Springs, Mississippi, on which his plan depended for food and materiel, was raided and burned by General Earl Van Dorn and his cavalry. Stores worth fifty million dollars in today's money were destroyed. Meanwhile in western Kentucky and western Tennessee, Lieutenant General Nathan Bedford Forrest and his cavalry were on a rampage, cutting telegraph lines and tearing up railroad track. With his supply lines cut and communication threatened, Grant saw that he would have to retreat. He sent word to Sherman that the assault of Vicksburg was off. But Sherman did not receive Grant's message for eight days. The story of this attempt on Vicksburg, like that of the entire war, is riddled with such incidents of messages gone astray, delayed, or ignored. The garrison commander at Holly

Springs was awakened with the news of Van Dorn's approach but went back to bed instead of mustering a defense.

When Pemberton heard from spies that Grant was in retreat, he ordered three brigades of infantry back to Vicksburg. No one knew precisely where Sherman was headed, but the Federals had provided a big clue several days before when the ironclad ship *Cairo* had ventured up the Yazoo River, where it was blown up by a mine. Its presence there indicated that the city might be attacked from the north. Heretofore, attention had been focused on threats from the south. Soon outposts upriver began sending messages of alarm to General Pemberton. Colonel Wirt Adams at Deer Creek (which fed into the Yazoo above Haines Bluff) sent word that "Forty-five of the enemy's transports, with troops, and ten gunboats passed Friar's Point on the 22d instant."[1] On December 24, the Yankee fleet was seen at Milliken's Bend. On Christmas Day, telegraph operator Phillip Fall, at DeSoto, wrote, "Sixty-four boats passed Transylvania which is 65 miles above here, at 11 o'clock last night. They ran with lights, at a rate of 18 miles an hour. There are now eighty-one boats between this and Lake Providence."[2] At 2 a.m. on Christmas Day, M. L. Smith at Vicksburg warned, "Sixty-four of the enemy's boats have passed Lake Providence to-night."[3]

On the twenty-sixth, Pemberton telegraphed Major J. R Waddy, the assistant adjutant-general at Jackson, forty miles east, "Push forward the troops as rapidly as possible. The enemy is landing."[4] He put Brigadier General Stephen Dill Lee[5]

---

[1] *OR*, ser. 1, vol. 17, pt. 2, p. 803.
[2] *OR*, ser. 1, vol. 17, pt. 2, p. 804.
[3] *OR*, ser. 1, vol. 17, pt. 2, p. 804.
[4] *OR*, ser. 1, vol. 17, pt. 2, p. 805.
[5] Stephen Dill Lee (1833–1908) was a South Carolinian, a West Pointer, and a veteran of the Mexican War as well as of the recent Virginia

in charge of defending the Chickasaw Bluffs on the northern edge of town, with 2,500 men to face 32,000 Federals. The bluffs gave them a height advantage, as did their gun emplacements. And then there was the terrain. In his report of the subsequent battle, Major General M. L. Smith described the bluff area with elegant precision:

> The broken ridge of hills touching the Mississippi at Vicksburg extends into the interior in nearly a direct line and has a direction at about right angles with the general course of the river. The Yazoo in its course touches the base of these hills at a point 12 miles in the interior known as Snyder's Mill; thence, diverging from them, empties into the Mississippi some 6 miles above the city. There is thus between the hills and the Yazoo a triangular-shaped area of bottom land, densely wooded, with the exception of one or two plantations on it, and intersected with bayous and low, swampy ground. Skirting the hills from Snyder's Mill down to near the Mississippi is first a swamp and then an old bed of the Yazoo, containing considerable water, and only to be crossed without bridging at three points, where torrents from the hills have borne along sufficient matter to fill up the bed. From the termination of this old bed to the Mississippi a belt of timber is felled, forming a heavy abatis. There was thus a continuous obstacle 12 miles long, formed of abatis and water, skirting the base of the hills and but a short distance from them, terminated at one end by our fixed batteries and fortified position at the mill; at the other end by the heavy batteries and field-works above Vicksburg. Through this obstacle there are but three natural passages.[6]

---

campaign. After the Civil War he became a Mississippi state senator and first president of the school known today as Mississippi State University.

[6] *OR*, ser. 1, vol. 17, pt. 1, p. 672.

The fate of the city and of large agricultural holdings outside it, as well as control of the river, hung on Sherman's being able to penetrate the morass. If he could storm the bluffs and secure them, he could also destroy the Vicksburg and Jackson Railroad, further isolating the city.

Brigadier General Stephen Dill Lee concluded that the Federals would probably land at or near Johnson's Plantation. He too saw the three ways they could approach the bluffs from there and deployed his men accordingly: at a place called the Sandbar, at an old Indian mound, and along a fork of Chickasaw Bayou. His analysis would soon be proven correct.

An old "friend" of Barton's Brigade was among the three Union divisions landing at the Johnson plantation on December 26: General George W. Morgan, whom they had chased out of Cumberland Gap. With him was Colonel John De Courcy, who had also played a role there and in the Battle of Tazewell. Private Robert Gorsuch of the 16th Ohio, whose diary had described the view from the Gap so well, was among the rank and file. At once Sherman sent out a reconnaissance party led by De Courcy. When the difference between the map and the actual landscape became clear, neither Morgan nor De Courcy believed the bluffs could be taken.

As all this was happening, Jefferson Davis was visiting Jackson, Mississippi, the state capital. On December 26, as Rebel troops were deploying in the trenches of the bluffs, he delivered a fire-breathing speech to the Mississippi legislature. After branding Northerners a separate race, inferior to Southerners, he defended his choice of Pemberton, a Philadelphian, to command at Vicksburg. He then described twenty-nine-year-old Brigadier General Stephen Lee. Said Davis,

> For the defense of Vicksburg, I selected one from the army of the Potomac of whom it is but faint praise to say he has no superior. He was sent to Virginia at the beginning

of the war, with a little battery of three guns. With these he fought the Yankee gunboats, drove them off, and stripped them of their terrors. He was promoted for distinguished services on various fields. He was finally made a colonel of cavalry, and I have reason to believe that, at the last great conflict on the field of Manassas, he served to turn the tide of battle and consummate the victory.[7]

That very day, Stephen Lee and his troops repulsed a Federal attack on the center of the Rebel line. That afternoon, the brigades of Barton, Gregg, and Vaughn began arriving by train. As part of the division commanded by General Stevenson, who had been with them at Cumberland Gap and through the invasion of Kentucky, the 40th, 42nd, and 43rd Georgia regiments arrived at Vicksburg on the twenty-seventh, with the 41st and 52nd following on the twenty-eighth, as John indicates in his correspondence. It was at Chickasaw Bayou that Barton's Brigade took the form it would maintain until the end of the war, bringing together the 40th, 41st, 42nd, 43rd, and 52nd north Georgia regiments. However, other units would be temporarily attached to these five regiments from time to time.

On December 27 and 28, Sherman made several attempts to take the bluffs, all repulsed with numerous casualties. Private Gorsuch noted tersely in his diary, "Sunday, December 28: Fighting this morning. We can hear the firing of both small arms and cannons plainly here on the boat....Several of the 16th killed...."[8] John's account of the 52nd in the Battle of Chickasaw Bayou begins on December 28.

---

[7] "Jefferson Davis: Address to the Mississippi Legislature, December 26, 1862," in Stephen W. Sears, ed., *The Civil War: The Second Year Told by Those Who Lived It* (New York: Library of America, 2012), 720–21.

[8] Gorsuch, *Civil War Diaries and Selected Letters*, 84.

January the 1 1863
Vicksburg Mississippi
Dear Companion
    I write you again to inform you that I am well at the present time hoping these lines will come to hand and find you all well they have been fighting here five or six days our boys have been to hard for them. So far we arrived at Vicksburg the 28th December at 11 oc we moved up the river two or three miles and set [?] up camp we stayed here until 8,oc at night when we moved a mile further and stoped in the road within less than half a mile of the enemy we lay here until the brake of day when we moved one or two hundred yards be [sic] behind the top of a hill here we lay until two hours of sun when we wer ordered to release a regiment that had been in our rifle pits for two or three days though the cannon had been roaring and the small armes firing

(2)

the whole day there were two men wounded close to me this was while we were behind the top of the hill there were nothing to be heard the whole day but the sound of gunes and the whzing of balls that passed over our heads when we left this place to go down to the breast works we went down a deep ravin or branch the banks of which was high enough to shelter us from the balls though they would come pretty close sometimes though we gotten to our trenches with out the loss of any men. There was but one man killed in our Regiment and one wounded the Enemy was fireing at us all this time we fired two three or four rounds at them done [illegible] for the next evning they come with a flag to bury there dead and there were nine within twenty-five steps of our entrenchments. Yesterday the 31st Dec they sent in for permission to bury there dead which was granted so there was not much fighting done yesterday we left the entrenchments this morning at day light and are tolerably pleasantly situated on the top of a high hill

(3)

within sight of the their batteries there is no fighting going on this morning as I can hear they have a large number of boats lying of two or thre miles in Yawzue river
though Vicksburg is on the Mississippi I will stop righting
about the fight for I might not right the truth as I know
but little about what was done out side of my own regiment. Yesterday morning after the flag of truce had been
sent out they came and hollowed to our boys and asked
them if they didn't want a dram so there was a good
maney questiones passed and finealy one of them agreed
to meet Captain Woodard[9] half way and take drink they
met and taken a dram swaped coat buttons V.C.[10]

I sent you my likeness from Atlanta which I hope you
have received before now—[11]

(4)

I received a leter and apir of Socks from you by the hand
of Lieutenant Underwood[12] when he come to camps and
also tell S, M, Douthit I received his letter And have not
had the chance To answer it give my compliments to all
inquiring friend and write your self direct your letters to
Vicksburg, Miss so nothing more at this time but remains
your husband until death.

John, M, Douthit

On the date of John's letter, Lincoln issued the Emancipation Proclamation. Letters from other Georgia soldiers
specify that they camped at Mint Springs Bayou, up the Yazoo

---

[9] Captain J. W. Woodward of John's company. After the war, he
would become editor of the *Dahlonega Signal* newspaper.

[10] I have not been able to determine what V.C. refers to.

[11] Only one photograph survives of John (included in this volume). It
probably is the photograph referred to in this letter, since he is in uniform.

[12] Lieutenant John E. Underwood of John's company. They enrolled
together at Morganton.

from Chickasaw Bayou. Today it is a part of the national military park, with two waterfalls and pleasant woods.

Like John, Ohio Private Gorsuch had but a sketchy understanding of the battle. His diary notes, "Monday, December 29, Batt--, ---[?]16th Regt. Cut to pieces Only 15 of Co. B got out....Tuesday, December 30 No fighting today. Both parties burying their dead. Rebels refuse to let us bury our dead who fell within their lines. They fire on our ambulances while taking away our dead and wounded. Wednesday December 31: Only 25 of our boys missing. Flag of truce went out and got the privilege to bury our dead. Feel very sick today. Our men planting siege guns...."[13]

Other accounts explain that the Confederates fired because it was too dark for them to see the truce flag. When it was light, they held their fire and allowed the Federals to retrieve the wounded and dead. Captain Rufus R. Asbury's diary indicates that he, too, participated in the friendly meeting John mentions.

Private Henry W. Robinson told his wife regarding the battle, "I never got tutch [touched] but the next time may be mine you doant no what kind of afeeling it put on me to See men Shot down like hoges & See aman tore all to peases with a Shell after he is dead...."[14] The report of General Barton, the brigade commander, gives a fuller view of the action.

Soon after my arrival here on the 27th I was ordered by Maj. Gen. M.L. Smith to take post with a part of my brigade on the road in rear of the rifle-pits on the lake some three miles north of the city, and take charge of the operations there. I found the post occupied by Colonel Morrison, with his regiment (Thirty-First Louisiana), a section of artillery, posted on an Indian mound in rear, all

---

[13] Gorsuch, *Civil War Diaries and Selected Letters*, 84.
[14] Robinson, January 2, 1863, letter.

supported by [Col. John A.] Rowan's Tennessee regiment on the road. The line of skirmishers to the right and left was strengthened and troops placed in position.

At 4:30 a.m. on the 28th the enemy opened with six pieces and sharpshooters on the works and road, and with few intermissions kept up his fire with increased force and vigor until night-fall. Rowan's regiment was sent early in the day to General Lee on his call for re-enforcements, and its place supplied by the Fortieth Georgia, Col. Abda Johnson. The rifle pits, sustaining a heavy fire and being threatened with assault, were re-enforced by five companies of this regiment, and two others strengthened the line of skirmishers. General Lee still needing troops, the Forty-second Georgia, Col. [R. J.] Henderson, was sent him, drawing the Third Tennessee from General Gregg, on my left to replace it.

During the afternoon the enemy having silenced the section on the mound, under fire of his artillery and infantry concentrated upon the breastworks, attempted to erect a battery at breaching distance. Major Ward with two sections, was ordered to engage the enemy's guns to [pre]vent this work. This was handsomely and successfully done and continued until darkness terminated the conflict. The night was passed strengthening the parapet and enlarging the work and rearranging and relieving the troops.

At daylight on the 29th the attack recommenced in heavy force, slackened in vigor about 7 a.m., but renewed about 11 a.m. and lasted until after dark. The enemy made five efforts to take the breastworks by storm—three times gained the crest of the parapet, once made a lodgment and attempted to mine, but on every occasion was repulsed with heavy loss. The Fifty-second Georgia, Col. [C. D.] Phillips, re-enforced the work early in the day. The line of skirmishers, formed by companies of the Fortieth and Forty-second Georgia, was earnestly engaged all day and held their position steadily and gallantly. The night was spent as before—in repairing the works and relieving the troops.

At daylight on the 30th the attack was renewed, but with less vigor, only three regiments and eight pieces of the enemy engaging the rifle-pits and skirmishers and a desultory fire was continued during the day. The enemy endeavored to erect batteries at various points, but was driven off.

I beg leave to call attention to the steadiness and intelligence of the troops under fire and the cheerfulness under the fatigues of three days and nights of incessant labor, watchfulness, and action.

My casualties amount to 15 killed and 39 wounded, exclusive of that of the Thirty first Louisiana of which no report has yet been received. The loss of the enemy can only be surmised, but was evidently heavy. Nearby, nine large grave-trenches, of capacity of 75 men each, were left filled. Hundreds were permitted to be carried off, and the ground for 150 yards in front of the breastworks gave frightful evidence of the great slaughter committed there. I estimate their killed, from these facts, at 650.[15]

Depending on who was counting, Barton had from 1,600 to 2,100 under his command at Chickasaw Bluffs.

Colonel C. H. Morrison of the 31st Louisiana said in his report, "During the hottest part of the engagement I was re-enforced on the left by the Fifty-Second Georgia Regiment, Colonel Phillips, to whom we were much indebted for the final repulse of the enemy."[16] He also praised the Georgia 40th for earlier relief.

After the war, Major Raleigh S. Camp of the Georgia 40th wrote, I believe that it is generally given up that if

---

[15] *OR*, ser. 1, vol. 17, pt. 1, p. 678.
[16] *OR*, ser. 1, vol. 17, pt. 1, p. 696.

Barton's Brigade had not arrived at the time it did that the Enemy would have dislodged Gen. Lee, and thus have taken the Stronghold Vicksburg. This fact is believed by all in the Brigade. And though the Genl Commanding has never said, officially as much, yet it is believed and any thing [we] may do to omit will not change the mind or remove the impression. It is fixed—this founded on truth.[17]

Later in the month, the *Southern Banner* reprinted from the *Vicksburg Whig* an unsigned letter that appears to be from a member of the Georgia 52nd. The writer objected that the *Whig* neglected to mention the exploits of the 52nd "in your notice of the fight of the 30th and 31st" and then corrected the record with his account of their service. He stated that the regiment "killed and wounded over fifteen to one in the fight of Monday." He corroborated John's description of starting above and going down a ravine to the breastworks during the engagement and described the heavy fire and casualties. He then went on to say that after the Federals left, skirmishers were sent out and "captured over a hundred shovels and axes, about twenty-five Minnie muskets, with accoutrements, about four hundred pounds of bacon, four boxes of soda biscuits, whisky, coffee and tea…. In scouting the woods we found about three hundred and fifty graves, in front of our rifle pits, and saw blood in every direction which proved that a great many had been wounded."[18] Despite the support of Porter's warships blasting at the bluffs, Sherman could not overcome the advantages given to the Confederates by the lay of the land

---

[17] Raleigh S. Camp, "What I Know I Know, and I Dare Express It': Major Raleigh S. Camp's History of the Georgia 40th Infantry in the Vicksburg Campaign," *Civil War Regiments* 5/1 (1996–1997): 52. In fact, General Pemberton did single out Georgia regiments for praise in his report.

[18] *Southern Banner* 31/47 (January 28, 1863): 2.

and by the withdrawal of Grant's army. His casualties were 1,779 compared to 187 Confederate deaths.

So far John had not seen much direct combat, but everything changed at the end of 1862. Though the war machine in the west was grinding slowly, it was grinding exceedingly fine. If the Georgia Brigade had not been ordered to Vicksburg, it would have been swept up in the bloody battle of Stones River, in which Bragg's Army of Tennessee met William Rosecrans's Army of the Cumberland near Murfreesboro and fought from December 31 to January 2. As it was, many of the brigade, by going instead to Vicksburg, bought only a few more weeks of life.

9

Protecting Gibraltar

Decades after the Civil War, Judge W. L. Calhoun gave a speech to the Confederate Veterans Association of Fulton County, Georgia, about his experiences as a captain in the Georgia 42nd at Vicksburg. The present tense used in his remarks might suggest that he was working from notes made while serving. To set the scene, he stated,

> Vicksburg is situated on the east bank of the Mississippi River, and is irregularly built on a range of hills rising successively from the river front; is picturesque and naturally a strong position. The river is about one mile wide and makes a bend, forming a considerable peninsula just opposite the city. It is well-fortified, there being on the river front a number of heavy siege guns, known as "water batteries"…consisting of eight six-inch columbiads;[1] one nine-inch Dahlgren; one eight-inch columbiad; one 7.44 Blakely gun; one 7 inch Brooks; one 6.4 inch Brooks, three smooth-bore 42 pounders; twenty-eight smooth-bore 32 pounders; eight banded and unbanded 32-pound rifles; one 18 pounder rifle; one 20-pounder Parrott; one Whitworth; one 10 inch mortar; one 8-inch howitzer—in all, 31 pieces of heavy artillery besides eighteen pieces of light artillery. Also a continuous line of entrenchments

---

[1] This is a mistake, as 6-inch columbiads were not manufactured by either side. Col. Edward Higgins's July 25, 1863, list of artillery he commanded on the batteries includes eight 10-inch columbiads and one 8-inch columbiad (*OR*, ser, 1, vol. 24, pt. 2, pp. 336–37).

with embrasures for artillery, entirely around the city, with heavy abattis in front wherever it could be constructed, and well-established picket posts on the hills outside of the main line. I thus found it when I arrived there just before day on the 31st of December, 1862.[2]

It is ironic that Vicksburg, a city of some 4,500 in 1860, with many trading ties to the north, had been pro-Union prior to Lincoln's call for troops in the aftermath of Ft. Sumter. Now it was the linchpin of Confederate resistance in the western theater.[3]

After Chickasaw Bayou, Barton's Brigade was not placed in Vicksburg proper but guarded a sector stretching from the Indian Mound at Chickasaw Bayou, where they had fought during the battle, to the race course nearby. They numbered 2,030 of the 20,856 in Stevenson's Division.[4] A short time later, General Barton was put in charge of defending Warrenton, a cotton town five miles south of Vicksburg not far from the plantations of Jefferson Davis and his brother.[5] Calhoun described the 42nd's later position: "afterwards below [Vicksburg] in the swamps, where from exposure, malaria, and bad and insufficient food, the men became almost walking skeletons."[6] What was true for the 42nd was, of course, true for the rest of the brigade.

---

[2] W. L. Calhoun, *The History of the 42nd Regiment, Georgia Volunteers, Confederate States Army, Infantry* (Atlanta: Sisson Printing, 1900), 29.

[3] See Peter F. Walker, *Vicksburg: A People at War, 1860–1865* (Chapel Hill, NC: University of North Carolina Press, 1960), for an examination of changing allegiances among Vicksburg residents.

[4] *OR*, ser. 1, vol. 24, pt. 3, p. 604. Stevenson noted in this January 25, 1863, document that not all of T. H. Taylor's regiments had arrived, so presumably they are not included in the total.

[5] The fortunes of Warrenton, original county seat of Warren County, changed when the Mississippi River changed its bed. Deprived of its port by this shift, it fell into decline and today is an unincorporated community.

[6] Calhoun, *History of the 42nd Regiment*, 30.

After repeatedly failing to take the city from the north by a variety of means, Grant had decided to attack Vicksburg from the south. He would bring his army far down the west bank of the Mississippi and send part of Admiral Porter's naval fleet past Vicksburg. If the boats survived the Vicksburg guns, he would then use them to transport the army across the river to the eastern bank, and march north from there. Although Memphis and New Orleans had fallen to the Union, the 240-mile stretch of river between Port Hudson and Vicksburg was still in Rebel hands.

The brigade was hardly in place around Warrenton before camp rumors as to the next posting began to swirl. Elation over the victory at Chickasaw Bayou had not lasted long. Writing on January 18 to his brother-in-law Redding Floyd, Matthias Murphy of Bartow County, Georgia, observed,

> The Yankees have all left this place and there is some such talk as we being ordered to Eastern Texas or to Savannah Georgia one or the other now in a short time...between me and you and the Gait post we have got the meanest Colonel in the Confederate service. Red the soldiers are all getting very tired of this war and if it is not stopt shortly they will stop it themselves by throughing down their muskets and going home. I am going to stay here till July Then if they do not let me come home on fair terms I am coming home on foul terms. This is worst place we have been camped at yet bad water bad beef and bad weather though I am fit as a bear.[7]

Murphy is speaking of Colonel Abda Johnson. When Barton took command of the Warrenton batteries, Johnson was given command of the brigade and would serve in that capacity until about May 10. According to Raleigh Camp, he

---

[7] A photocopy of the original is in McCardle Research Library, Old Vicksburg Courthouse.

acquitted himself well.[8] At Champion Hill, despite being gravely ill, Johnson insisted on staying with his men. In any event, complaints home have always provided the momentary relief that helped soldiers to continue to perform their duties.

As usual, John writes without heat.

Feb.2, 1863
Camped near Vicksburg, Miss.
Dear Companion
    I now take my pen in hand to drop you a few lines which will inform you that I am well at this time hoping these lines will come to hand and find you all enjoying the same like blessing I do not know that I have anything to write that will interest you We have moved from where we were camped when I last wrote We are camped now about two miles be low Vicksburg Our former camps being above the enemy is still in sight that is their boats They are trying to cut or open the canal below the place so they can get below without having to pass our heavyest guns They may pass with there gun boats and there hole fleet if they get the canal open They passed our batteries with one gun boat this morning our guns firing at her all the while how often they struck her I do not know. Those that saw her says she went through in a hury If they get possession of the river be low there Vicksburg will be of little importance to us but be fore they injure us very bad they will have to take fort Hudson some two hundred miles be low here though they have stopped our transportation be[tween] [illegible]

[page 2]
    And fort Hudson The weather is very warm and wet here and mud here. There is no end to it You need not send me my clothes now if you could without it is some

---

[8] Camp, "What I Know…," 53.

socks as we have drawed clothing I do not know how long we will stay here I hope we will not have to stay here through the summer. I hope the war will end so I can get to come home and stay next summer I would be glad to see you all and think I will get to come home and see you all this spring I want you to be shure and write for I have received but one letter from you since I have been here and it was dated in December Give my best respects to your father and family So nothing more but remains your husband until death

John, M, Douthit

The gunboat John refers to was the Union ram, *Queen of the West*, commanded by nineteen-year-old Colonel Charles Rivers Ellet, one of six Ellets serving in the Union navy and son of the engineer Charles Ellet, Jr., the man responsible for introducing the naval ram into the Union navy. Admiral Porter ordered Ellet to destroy the steamer *City of Vicksburg*, moored at Vicksburg. Because preparations took longer than expected, the *Queen* had to operate in daylight rather than in pre-dawn darkness and was shelled the whole time she was trying to attack the steamer. She got away without permanent damage to herself despite taking twelve direct hits. The *City of Vicksburg* caught fire and was heavily damaged but did not founder. Ellet showed that a fast-moving boat could run the Vicksburg batteries. As soon as the *Queen* could be repaired, Admiral Porter ordered Ellet to wreak havoc farther south. Ellet reported to Porter from below Vicksburg on February 5, "At Warrenton...the enemy had two batteries, of four pieces each, of which four are 20-pounder rifled guns. They opened fire upon us as we passed, but only struck us twice, doing no injury."[9] This is probably the encounter John describes. Later in his report, Ellet states that on the way back upriver he

---

[9] *OR*, ser. 1, vol. 24, pt. 1, p. 338.

found that the Warrenton batteries had increased to three; but again, they did little damage to the *Queen*. "Fort Hudson" was actually heavily fortified Port Hudson, whose guns challenged any Union boats coming up from New Orleans. The *Queen of the West* destroyed a great many supplies destined for Port Hudson and captured several steamers before being captured itself. The canal being dug across the peninsula was one of Grant's several failed attempts to circumvent the big guns of Vicksburg.

Winter rains were heavy in January. Others of the brigade mentioned in letters that they had no tents until January 22. They dug holes in a hillside and covered the openings with boards to get out of the water and mud. As for food, Private Patrick Stovall of the Georgia 40th wrote that the beef "ain't got more grease in it, than a piece of wood."[10] On January 28, the brigade's supply wagons from Tennessee finally arrived.

> Vicksburg
> Feb 8 1863
> Dear Wife
>
> Your kind favor of the 23rd of Jan was received today and gave me a real joy for nothing pleases me better than to hear that all is well at home You need not send me any clothing for I do not need any thing unless it is one pair of socks and if Mr. John Hicks wants pay for bringing them you need not send them by him. I do not need socks very bad I draw plenty of clothing and have now as much as I can toat on a march I received the braids of hair you sent and would be a great deal better pleased to see the heads they came off of but that cannot be yet awhile but I hope the time will speedily pass off when the way worn

---

[10] Quoted in Goodson, "Part II—Letters and Diaries," *Georgia Confederate 7,000*, 49.

[page 2]
and war worn soldiers may find repose in the bosom of an
affectionate family The Yankees are a cross the river and
have been there for a month But there is no prospect of a
fight soon. We get good rations of corn meal beef sugar
molasses and have tents to lay in. My health is very good.
I am affectionately and only yours

John M Douthit

Military records show that John Hicks, of Company H,
was AWOL for two months in early 1863. Since he was illiterate, he would not have had the consolation of correspondence and had either deserted or gone home on a visit to see
how his family was faring. He may have returned to his regiment under duress. On January 25, Captain Gus Boyd and
four other officers, including John's cousin-in-law Alfred
Weaver, were sent back to Fannin County to recruit new men
and round up deserters. Hicks would be killed at Baker's
Creek in the retreat from Champion Hill on May 16, leaving
a widow, Susan, in Morganton.

By now Baby Victoria was seven months old, perhaps
with enough hair for a tiny braid. Her sister Julitty was two
years and seven months old. Martha might also have sent a
braid of her own hair. In 1863 John's letters gradually grow
shorter and he appears less interested in relaying information.
Homesickness, illness, and the deaths of fellow soldiers must
have weighed heavily on him. Many of the friends and neighbors he signed up with had died or deserted. March was a busy
month on the river, with the Union probing for control and a
way to get at Vicksburg, but John says almost nothing about
these efforts. While it is true that he seldom reports on anything but his own, direct experience, one is reminded of the
spare letters written during his illness at Strawberry Plains.

March 1, 1863
My Dear Companion,
    As it has been Three weeks since I have written you a letter I take my pen in hand to drop you a few lines this morning which will inform you that I am well at the present time hoping these few lines will come to hand and find you all well, I have nothing strange to write you at this time The enemy's fleet is still in sight They throw Boomes [bombs] occasionally in to the City but do little or no damage They may attact us here again but I hardly think they will I want them to do what they are going to do for I want to get away from this place Spring has come and the farmers are planting here and when it is not raining it is very warm here I want you to write to me for I have [not] received an answer to the first letter that I wrote since I come to this place you either don't write or your leters don't come to hand (rest of the letter missing).

John's good health was not to last. His medical record shows that he was sick with diarrhea on March 14. As always, he made little of it. Not so Henry Robinson, who also was stricken early in 1863 and gave some idea of what the suffering was like: "I taken the Dyhoree the nite after I Rote to you [wife Elizabeth] & amondy morning before day I took a thowing up & I was worket both ways til I had nothing but water in me but I field Some better to day...."[11] A month later he added, "I haven't bin abel to do eny duty for 2 weaks or more I have the dyorhee & eat nothing til I cant hardley walk I have fell away 21 lbs. cence I came heare...."[12] In his February 11 letter, he mentions being given quinine and mourns, "I have kild my Self a marching & carring So much in my knapsack." He also poignantly described the feelings many there

---

[11] Robinson, letter, January 6, 1863.
[12] Robinson, letter, February 6, 1863.

contended with: "...when I ly down at nite my brest all filled with immotion half smothered & chockt & half sleeping & half dreaming all nite & when I git up in the morning I am worse worred then when I ly down witch leaves a man un fit fur duty & very un hapy...."[13] Robinson died "of disease" April 12.

March the 19ᵗʰ 1863
Dear Companion
I write you again to let you know that I am still al[ive] though not well but I am mending and think if I get no back set I will be well in a few days hoping these lines will come to hand and find you well I have nothing new to write you at this time I have write[n] so much and get no letters I [am?] almost out of heart of writing but I will write as long as there is any hopes of your getting the letters that I send you. You can not imag[ine] how I want to be at home so that I can get something that I could eat the most I have eaten for several da[ys] has been milk for which I gave fifty cents per quart and buter at two dollars per pound. Davis Douthit is in moderate health though I don't think he will stand ca[mp?] life so I will close by signing my na[me]
Your husband until death
John M Douthit

The purchasing power of $.50 in 2017 money would be $9.73. John's younger brother, Warren Davis Douthit, is not listed in regimental histories (though he does have a service record), so it is important to see him show up here in this letter. The recruiting/rounding-up trip of Captain Boyd may have snared him or he may have volunteered. On February 8, Davis filed his will at the Fannin County courthouse, leaving

---

[13] Robinson, letter, February 16, 1863.

everything to his wife, as John had done just before he signed up. The language of the document was the same as in John's will. It was witnessed by his brother Solomon and three relatives of his wife. John shows no great joy in having Davis with him. Perhaps he expressed this in a lost letter; but more probably, John was sad to see his younger brother caught up in a war for which the family had never felt much enthusiasm. By now, John had been in the army over a year.

By the time John wrote again, Grant, after more failed attempts to approach Vicksburg, had formed a promising plan to get his troops across the Big Muddy some forty miles to the south. On March 31, McClernand's and McPherson's divisions were on the march to Bruinsburg, where they would eventually cross.

> In Camps, Near Vicksburg, Miss.
> April the 7th 1863
> Dear Companion
>
> I this morning take my pen in hand to write you a few lines which will inform you that I am well at this time, hoping these lines will come to hand and find you all well. I have nothing new or strange to write. I received a letter from you some days ago bearing date of March the [illegible] which gave me much satisfaction to hear from you one time more as it seems like you have all quit writing. I want to come home and see you all but have give out getting to come this spring but I intend coming the first opportunity but the Lord onley Knows when that will be. So you must do the best you can and not get out of heart for I hope I will live to see the close of this cruel war and enjoy many pleasant days afterward with my friends and family. If you see Harriet you can tell Her that Davis is in common health, Tell Mother Douthit that Uncle Jack McClure, Harrison McClure, Thomas Bly and Michum Gallaway are here and was well the last time I saw them.

Give my respets to all inquiring friends so I will close hoping to hear from you soon So nothing more at present onley remains your affectionate husband until death John, M, Douthit

P.S. Since writing the above I have received two letters from you dated the 20 and 29 of March which gave me great satisfaction to hear from you and to hear that you was well. So adieu my Dear Martha

On the day John found his brother "in common health," Davis was diagnosed with "rheumatism," as were almost ten thousand others in the Army of Tennessee between June 1862 and May 1863.[14] Frank Freemon suggests this diagnosis most often referred to joint pain resulting from strenuous physical activity.[15] The McClures and Galloways were probably relatives. John's mother was a McClure and her sister had married a Galloway. Davis's wife Harriet was listed as illiterate in the 1860 census, so John was passing news of him to her through Martha.

Vicksburg Miss Aprile the 16th 1863
Dear Companion

I this morning take my pen in hand to let you know that I am in common health at this time hoping these lines will come to hand and find you all well. I have nothing new to write you at this time I received two letters from you not very long since which I was glad to hear from you. There is no prospect of fighting here nor of our leaving here as I know of, The weather is very warm here when it is dry and when it is raining tolerable cool. If you see Harriett tell here that Davis is not very stout if the cow that Harriett has will do here any good let here keep here

---

[14] Cunningham, *Doctors in Gray*, 205.

[15] Frank R. Freemon, *Gangrene and Glory: Medical Care During the American Civil War* (Urbana, IL: University of Illinois Press, 2001), 233.

that is if you do not need here your self. So do the best you can until this cruel war ends. So nothing more at present onley remains your husband until death

John, M, Douthit

On the date of this letter, Admiral Porter began sending gunboats and transports past the river batteries, so that boats would be available to ferry the divisions of McClernand and McPherson across the Mississippi. On April 22, John's medical record shows that he was again ill with diarrhea. Whether the diarrhea indicated dysentery, food poisoning, or some other illness is not stated. Confederate surgeon Joseph Jones wrote, "Chronic diarrhoea and dysentery were the most abundant and most difficult to cure amongst army diseases; and whilst the more fatal diseases, as typhoid fever, progressively diminished, chronic diarrhoea and dysentery progressively increased, and not only destroyed more soldiers than gunshot wounds, but more soldiers were permanently disabled and lost to the service from these diseases than from the disability following the accidents of battle."[16] Today, the "cures" seem quaint if not bizarre. They included cauterization of several inches of the mucus membrane of the rectum, injections of silver nitrate, administering such drugs as opium, calomel, and acetate of lead for diarrhea, and a host of plant materials—blackberry leaves, black oak, resin, red pepper—these last seen as astringents.[17]

---

[16] Quoted in Cunningham, *Doctors in Gray*, 185–86.
[17] Cunningham, *Doctors in Gray*, 187.

Vicksburg Miss April the 30th 1863

Dear Companion I write you a few lines I am in common health at this time hoping these lines will find you all well I have but little time to write as I expect to send this letter to Atlanta to be mailed by Lieut McClure[18] the rail road is torn up between here and there that we get no regular mail nor don't send out any So I have to close I will write more as soon as the mail gets to running So nothing more onley remains Your husband until death [unsigned]

The railroad tracks had just been wrecked by cavalry under the command of Colonel Benjamin Grierson, who before the war had been a music teacher in Jacksonville, Illinois. Grierson and his men rode out of La Grange, Tennessee, on April 17 and, as part of a sixteen-day, six-hundred-mile raid that took them all the way to Baton Rouge, disabled both the Mobile & Ohio Railroad and the Southern Railroad and destroyed telegraph lines, rolling stock, supplies destined for Vicksburg, and much else. They aimed to provide a diversion that would take General Pemberton's attention away from Grant's maneuvers. Van Dorn's cavalry, which might have caught up with Grierson, was on loan to Bragg in Tennessee. On the date of this letter, McPherson's and McClernand's troops crossed at Bruinsburg. Grant's push north began, and on May 1, Port Gibson fell to superior Union numbers.

On May 2, John was diagnosed with remit fever. This term, or *remittent fever*, refers to a fever that comes and goes. That description could fit a number of diseases. But Freemon

---

[18] Robert N. McClure was the only Lieutenant McClure in Barton's Brigade at that time. His February 2 resignation due to disability (persistent edema in the legs) was approved by the regimental surgeon. Perhaps the torn-up railroad tracks kept him in Warrenton long enough to take the mail to Georgia in April.

notes that the diagnosis of remittent fever "may have included a few patients with another type of infection, but most patients with this diagnosis had malaria; we know this because remittent fever had the same seasonal and regional variations as malaria and because it responded to quinine."[19] Not only were the Vicksburg environs swampy and netted with bayous, but Grant's efforts to dig canals created areas of standing water that bred malaria-bearing mosquitoes. The weeks of incessant rain made it all worse. If John had malaria, he would have experienced chills, fever, nausea, vomiting, headaches, and fatigue. Evidently the worst symptoms had not yet hit, for he was able to write to Martha again.

> May the 2nd 1863
> Vicksburg Miss
> Dear Companion
> I write you a few lines to let you know that I am still alive and in Common health hoping these lines will come safe to hand and find you all well. I started a few lines to you and sent it out by Lieut McClure a few days ago The rail road is torn up so the mail don't go out nor come in Consequently we have had no mail in several days and have not written any letters for some time which will account for your getting no mail. There is considerable excitement here at this time. There have been was some fighting below here yesterday in which we got the best of it We are expecting to leave here
> (2)
> this eavning or in the morning to go below though we may not go. We just got in this morning from above we went up five or six miles above Vicksburg night before last it was reported the Enemy was landing up there. It is thought here they will attack us both above and below and

---

[19] Freemon, *Gangrene and Glory*, 206.

in the center all at the same time. And if they do we may have some tolerable hot work to do. I have subscribed for a news paper printed at this place which if you get it Regular will give you most of the news about this place. I will send this by the hand of Wm Blalock I will also send you fifty dollars in it which you will use to the best advantage you can. I will say to you do the Best you can with your stock. The Lord onley knows whether I will ever live to get home or not But I shall live in hopes

(3)

As long as I live at all. Tell Harriett that Davis is in common health he is getting a goodeal stouter than he has been. I think he will get stout enough to make a very good soldier all without it is on long marches. I don't think he will s[t]and a hard march. Charley Hennson is some better than he has been. Write to me when these lines come to hand and let me know how you are getting along and let me know whether you get the money or not Give my best respects to all inquiring friends I think the train will be running through in a few days so we can get our mail.

Here the original stops at a ragged edge. On the photocopy, someone has typed this ending: "So I will close. Nothing more only remain your husband until death. John M. Douthit." Possibly these lines were written on the back and discovered after the photocopy was made.

Charlie Henson may have arrived with John's brother Davis. He enlisted in Co. H. of the 52nd on February 12, 1863. A William Blaylock served in the Georgia 39th infantry, Company E, made up of north Georgia troops from Walker County. The second brigade under General Carter Stevenson, like the first (Barton's Brigade), consisted of Georgia regiments, including the 39th. With the 52nd, they started out at Camp McDonald, served in east Tennessee, in the invasion of Kentucky, and in middle Tennessee before Vicksburg.

To take attention away from the crossing at Bruinsburg, Grant ordered Sherman to send troops and gunboats up the Yazoo River to feint at the fortifications of Snyder's Bluff. The need to continue fortifying the bluffs above Vicksburg stretched Pemberton's forces thin. Sherman sent two-thirds of his men south to aid Grant while the other third pretended to be crossing the river above the city at Snyder's Bluff. He thus provided an additional diversion, besides Grierson's raid, and drew Rebels "five or six miles above Vicksburg," as John reports. Sherman kept up the ruse from April 29 to May 1. The "fighting below" that John refers to was the Battle of Port Gibson, in which 6,000 Rebels inflicted serious damage but fell, contrary to John's understanding, to 23,000 Federals. Now Grant's army was steadily closing in on the Gibraltar of the West.

John was correct to send newspapers to Martha, for even generals sometimes read them to find out what was going on. Sherman, who hated reporters and considered them no better than spies, blamed his defeat at Chickasaw Bayou on journalists who published his plans before he could put them into action. This time, however, no news stories changed the odds and Sherman's diversion worked. With more Union troops arriving below Vicksburg by the hour, Grant was poised to put enormous pressure on the city one way or another.

May the 6th 1863
Vicksburg Miss
Dear Companion I write you again to let you know that I am still alive and in common health at this time hoping thes lines will find you all well so I have nothing very strange to write you at this time. I received aletter from you yesterday bearing date of April the 18th which I was glad to receive as it was the first that I had received for several days though I could not expect letters to come

when there was no mail, the mail was stoped on account of the rail Road being torn up you stated that you had not heard from me in some time I wrote reggular until as long as the mail went through and sent a few lines by Lieut. Mcclure to

[page 2]

be mailed at Atlanta I started you a letter with fifty dollars in it to you by Wm. Blalock two or three days ago The Regiment left here day before yesterday they are now ten miles below here at warrenton I did not feel very stout and the doctor said I had better not go so I am still here but think I will go to the Regiment to morrow or next day as for war news there is plenty here but I suppose you can hear plenty of that with out my writing any. Though you may listen for a big fight from this place before long in this country So nothing more onely Remains your husband, until death John, M, Douthit write soon and often

Whether or not John was ever completely well after this letter, we do not know. But the end game for Vicksburg had started. According to Raleigh Camp, the brigade left Warrenton on the night of Saturday, May 2. They "marched nearly all night crossing the Big Black just before day at Hankerson's Ferry"[20] some fourteen miles from Warrenton. By Monday the fourth they would have fallen back to Warrenton, where John could have joined them for the run-up to Champion Hill.

---

[20] Camp, "What I Know…," 55–56.

10

Champion Hill[1]

On May 1, General Pemberton moved his headquarters from Jackson, the Mississippi capital, into Vicksburg. Jefferson Davis had ordered Pemberton to defend the river city at all costs, so Pemberton's mindset was defensive, not offensive.[2] His objective was to keep his army between Grant's army and Vicksburg. In the early part of Grant's march north to take "Gibraltar," Pemberton arraigned his troops behind the Big Black River, a waterway that originates in north central Mississippi and flows southwest to join the Father of Waters twenty-five miles south of Vicksburg, forming a natural line of defense.

As Barton's Brigade was stationed at Warrenton below Vicksburg (and behind the Big Black), they and the rest of Carter L. Stevenson's Division stood between the southern edge of the city and Grant's advancing army; or so Pemberton thought. But Grant did not march directly up the river as expected. He avoided both heavily garrisoned Warrenton and the forces holding the eighty-foot-high railroad bridge over the Big Black River in favor of angling in a northeasterly direction to cut the Southern Railroad at Edwards Station, be-

---

[1] As noted in the preface, no letter from John Douthit concerning the Battle of Champion Hill survives. Therefore, this chapter is meant to sketch events that John and his brother Davis would have participated in or observed. It does not pretend to give a full treatment of the battle but will serve to continue John's story.

[2] Davis called Vicksburg the "nailhead" that held the two halves of the Confederacy together.

tween Jackson and Vicksburg. Doing so would deprive Vicksburg of supplies from the bulk of the Confederacy.

Pemberton believed Grant's march towards Edwards Station to be a ruse and suspected that Grant would turn towards the bridge spanning the Big Black in order to cross it and attack Vicksburg; and he planned for that. But on May 12, after the Federals were victorious over a smaller Rebel force at tiny Raymond, Grant revised his plans again. He would set his sights on taking Jackson, forty-five miles east of Vicksburg, before he dealt with the latter, despite the fact that this would place his army between two Confederate forces: Pemberton, who on May 12 moved his headquarters to Bovina, seven miles east of Vicksburg, and the newly arrived Joseph E. Johnston, commander of the Department of the West, at Jackson.

It was a risky move, but as Timothy Smith notes in his book about the Battle of Champion Hill, Grant correctly surmised that both commanders would "react passively"[3] and not attack him. Pemberton, worried about the Southern Railroad, ordered first General John Bowen's Division, then William Loring's and Stevenson's, to march for Edwards Station, not quite halfway to Jackson. All told, he would assemble around 22,000 men there, leaving 7,500 to guard Vicksburg and another 3,000 spread out to guard roads and bridges.[4] John and his brother Davis, we assume, were two of the 22,000. The US forces numbered about 32,000 on May 15.

In Jackson, hearing of Grant's approach (with Sherman on the way to join him), Johnston sent a telegram to Jefferson Davis—"I am too late"—then ordered the city evacuated and

---

[3] Timothy B. Smith, *Champion Hill: Decisive Battle for Vicksburg* (New York: Savas Beatie, Civil War Preservation Trust Special Edition, 2007), 88.

[4] Winston Groom, *Vicksburg* (New York: Alfred A. Knopf, 2009), 313.

fled north, leaving a relatively small force under Brigadier General John Gregg to cover his retreat. The brave Gregg had already tried to stem the blue tide at Raymond.

On a rainy May 14, the Federals easily took Jackson. That done, Grant ordered Sherman to destroy anything useful to the Rebel army and turned the rest of his troops to face Vicksburg some thirty-five miles to the west. In the critical events that followed, Pemberton was tasked with serving two masters—President Davis and General Johnston, who did not like each other. Davis urged defense, Johnston offense, as long as it did not involve him. One is reminded of Grant's remark that if there are two generals in the field, that is one too many. Pemberton also was losing the support of his subordinates. Some, perhaps, had never trusted this northerner who had married into the southern cause. Moreover, his generals disagreed among themselves as to the next step. When Pemberton called a council of war, some wanted to meet the enemy and fight, Pemberton wanted to pull the troops on the march back across the Big Black to defend Vicksburg, and some—such as Loring and Stevenson—favored cutting Grant's supply line between Jackson and Grand Gulf to the southeast. All the while, Pemberton believed that reinforcements would come, as he had sent several appeals for help. But the troops never arrived, for General Johnston withdrew his troops before they had a chance to fight. Johnston sent word that Pemberton should march to join him.

Loring's plan won the day. A hard rain on the fourteenth had softened the ground, complicating all movement. Early on May 15, Pemberton sent the army down a road they had not scouted. There were aggravating delays. Someone had forgotten that there was not much food and ammunition at Edwards Station. No one checked Baker's Creek after the rain; the crossing was flooded. Stevenson's division, including Barton's Brigade, did not leave Edwards Station until about 5 p.m. W.

L. Calhoun commented, "I shall never forget this tiresome march; our division having arrived upon what, in a few hours was the field of a bloody battle, at midnight, very much fatigued."[5] It was 3 a.m. before the last troops, at the end guarding the wagons, were allowed to sleep. Carter Stevenson's 12,000-man division, the largest under Pemberton's command, had been marching next to the wagons. Besides the First, or Barton's Brigade, Stevenson's division included the Second Brigade, commanded by Brigadier General Stephen D. Lee of Chickasaw Bayou note; the Third Brigade, under Brigadier General Alfred Cumming;[6] the Fourth, under Colonel Alexander W. Reynolds;[7] and an artillery unit commanded by Major Joseph W. Anderson.[8] Fatigue and lack of sleep would play a part in the events to come.

Early the next day, General Johnston, who was marching away from both Jackson and Vicksburg, sent new orders telling Pemberton to join him at Clinton. Before the directive could be fully implemented, sounds of artillery fire were heard. The fighting that would revolve around a hill on Sid Champion's estate had started. The hill, which rose some 140 feet from an uneven terrain of farmland and woods, would change

---

[5] Calhoun, *History of the 42nd Regiment*, 31.

[6] Brigadier General Alfred Cumming (1829–1910), a native Georgian and West Point graduate, served with distinction in Virginia early in the war and was wounded at Malvern Hill. After Vicksburg, he was active in such actions as the Atlanta Campaign and Missionary Ridge.

[7] Col. Alexander W. Reynolds (1816–1876), Virginia native and West Point graduate, served in the Mexican War. During the Civil War he served under Kirby Smith in eastern Tennessee before Vicksburg. Afterward, he fought at Chattanooga and Atlanta. He ended his career in the Egyptian army.

[8] Major Joseph Washington Anderson (1835–1863) had originally commanded the Botetourt Artillery and led it in eastern Tennessee and in the invasion of Kentucky. He was Stevenson's chief of artillery now and would not survive the day.

hands three times during the battle. Champion himself was away, serving with the 28th Mississippi Cavalry. His wife Matilda and children would hide in the cellar during the fight.[9] After the siege of Vicksburg, Sherman burned the house. As Winston Groom summarizes the situation of Pemberton's forces, "So after first having faced south to cut a Federal supply line, then reversing itself to face north for the union with Johnston, the Confederate army now turned east to face U.S. Grant."[10] This meant, for starters, that the 400-wagon train of supplies that brought up the rear of Stevenson's division was now at the head. Carter Stevenson immediately charged the Fourth Brigade, under Colonel A. W. Reynolds, with reversing the train and clearing the road for troop movement.

On that day, May 16, the day of the battle that came to be known as Champion Hill or Baker's Creek, a correspondent for a Cincinnati newspaper saw the terrain this way: "The rebels having the choice of position, selected for their battlefield the most advantageous ground within several miles of Edwards Station. They made a good selection, as they always do. To reach their lines from the road on which we were travelling, our men had to cross two open fields and ascend a steep slope, exposed to their fire from the woods, and unable to return it so as to do execution. It was the best position for defence that they have selected in Mississippi yet."[11]

---

[9] Rebecca Blackwell Drake and Margie Riddle Bearss, *My Dear Wife: Letters to Matilda; the Civil War Letters of Sid and Matilda Champion*, no place, no publisher, third printing, 2006, p. 59. This source, based on material discovered in 2007, contradicts earlier stories that Matilda Champion fled with her children.

[10] Groom, *Vicksburg*, 322.

[11] Frank Moore, ed., Cincinnati "Commercial" Account, *Rebellion Record: A Diary of American Events*, vol. 6 (New York: G.P. Putnam, 1863), 617.

South of Champion Hill, the aforementioned "steep slope," Carter Stevenson ordered the rest of his division to form a line of battle in the crossroads area, where the Jackson, Middle, and Raymond roads came together. He had been charged with holding the crossroads. Within Stevenson's Division, as combat began that morning, Seth Barton and his Georgians were on the right of the line, Alfred Cumming north of him in the center, and the experienced Stephen Lee at the head of several Alabama regiments past Cumming, on the left, where he had taken the position vacated by Reynolds when the wagons were moved. The line was facing roughly east, with the left (Lee) resting where the roads came together and the other two brigades positioned down the Raymond Road. Grant was traveling towards the Champion Hill area from the east by three roughly parallel roads.

Meanwhile, Grant, from a position on Champion Hill, ordered his troops to engage about 10:30. When Stephen Lee became aware of Federals (Hovey's division) approaching from the north, he moved towards Champion Hill to meet them and sent a message to Cumming, asking him to fill the gap in defense he was creating by moving away from the crossroads. Stevenson approved Lee's move; the guns on Champion Hill needed infantry support. Not long after this, Cumming, who had assumed command of his brigade only a few days before, positioned the 56th and 57th Georgia to guard the crossroads and moved with the rest of his troops (the 34th, 36th, and 39th Georgia regiments) north of the Middle Road. This created an L-shape in Stevenson's line. Cumming and Lee were turned north towards the approaching Federals. The two regiments at the crossroads and Barton, south of the crossroads on the Raymond Road, continued to face east. Stevenson's left flank (Lee and Cumming) would have to keep turning to meet the advancing enemy. In the melee of the day, a gap formed

between Lee and Cumming; and the crossroads was left lightly (but vigorously) defended.

In his report of the battle, filed July 29 from Demopolis,
Alabama, Carter Stevenson stated of subsequent events,
"Finding [the enemy] were about to concentrate on the left
with the larger part of their force, still moving a column to the
flank, as I had no reserve, I moved General Barton (my right
brigade) by the rear to the extreme left."[12] Stevenson felt the
shift "was necessary to protect the right and rear of the new
line, now threatened by [the Raymond and Clinton] roads."[13]
The new line "was necessarily single, irregular, divided, and
without reserves. Under the supposition that the army was to
move forward in pursuance of the instructions given in the
morning, this ground was not reconnoitered with a view to
taking up a position for battle until we were on the move facing the enemy."[14] In this configuration, the right was occupied
by Cumming's Brigade. Lee's Brigade of Alabamans held the
center, and Barton's Brigade was on the left and stretched towards Baker's Creek, near the upper crossing. The immediate
goal was to keep the Federals from getting between Pemberton's army and Edwards Depot. All the while, Stevenson tried
to keep Pemberton informed of events and several times asked
for reinforcements to counter the superior numbers of the
Federals.

Around 10:30 a.m., Lee and Cumming were attacked by
a much larger force and were initially pushed back. The fight
seesawed and Lee counter-attacked around noon. Meanwhile,
Barton had been hurrying to the left. By the time he arrived, it
was too late; Lee's flank had been turned. Furthermore, as he
noted in his own report of the battle, "The position was not a

---

[12] *OR*, ser. 1, vol. 24, pt. 2, p. 94.
[13] *OR*, ser. 1, vol. 24, pt. 2, p. 94.
[14] *OR*, ser. 1, vol. 24, pt. 2, p. 95.

good one; the country much broken and covered in most parts with dense woods."[15] He also was down in numbers, having been directed earlier to send one regiment and a section of artillery to hold the bridge over Baker's Creek. The 42nd Georgia and a section of the Mississippi Artillery were chosen. Nevertheless, the brigade joined the fray with alacrity. Barton reported,

> With impetuous gallantry the Fortieth, Forty-first, and Forty-Third Georgia Regiments dashed upon the enemy's line, broke it, and drove it back about 300 yards. It was here re-enforced by his second and third lines, and my farther advance was checked. I had reserved the Fifty-second on the left to protect that flank; it was now moved up rapidly, and in handsome style engaged a brigade that was turning the left. The troops on the right now gave way, and my right flank was soon turned and overwhelmed. The left was in like manner enveloped and a heavy fire poured in from the rear. Having vainly endeavored to cover the left with the Forty-Second Regiment, brought forward for the purpose, I was compelled to fall back. The enemy had so nearly surrounded the whole brigade that this movement was necessarily accompanied with some confusion. The Fortieth and Forty-second Regiments, however, came out with unbroken ranks. The brigade had been terribly handled.[16]

Barton was not aware when he attacked Smith's advance that John Stevenson's Ohio and Illinois regiments were approaching to his left and he would thus soon be surrounded.

Corput's battery, which had six guns, was aided by the 52nd Georgia and the 1st Mississippi Light Artillery in holding back swarms of Federals. Around 2:30 p.m., Bowen's division came up to aid Cumming and Lee, and the tide turned in

---

[15] *OR*, ser. 1, vol. 24, pt. 2, p. 99.
[16] *OR*, ser. 1, vol. 24, pt. 2, p. 100.

the middle. As Stevenson described Barton's fate, "In the mean time the enemy had continued his movement to our left, and fell upon Barton in overwhelming numbers. He charged them gallantly, but was forced back, and the enemy, following up his advantage, cut him off entirely from the rest of the division."[17] Major Anderson, chief of artillery, was killed, and Corput's, Johnston's, and Waddell's batteries were lost. Almost all the artillery horses were killed. Colonel Phillips, leader of the 52nd, wounded in four places, would be listed as missing at the end of the day. He would survive to spend months at the Federal prison or Johnson's Island, Ohio, from which he was paroled on February 24, 1865.[18] Captain W. W. Brown of Company H was shot in both legs. The brigade's line crumbled and soldiers retreated in confusion. Later, commanders argued about who broke first. But there was nothing to do but retreat. Barton's men had charged forward too fast, enabling John Stevenson to cut them off from the rear. Of the day's events Carter Stevenson would conclude bitterly, "The non-arrival of re-enforcements for my division early in the day, in my opinion, was mainly the cause of our failure. As to the reason therefor it is not for me to express an opinion here."[19]

During the retreat that ensued, there were attempts to reform and make a stand, but only Stephen Lee seemed able to rally his troops. Barton noted mildly, "I retired across Baker's Creek, posting the few troops remaining so as to command the bridge."[20] He was speaking of the upper crossing of the creek. Many of his men used the lower crossing as they fled in

[17] *OR*, ser. 1, vol. 24, pt. 2, p. 95.
[18] Lillian Henderson, *Roster of the Confederate Soldiers of Georgia, 1861–1865*, vol. 5 (Hapeville, GA: Longino & Porter, 1960), 448.
[19] *OR*, ser. 1, vol. 24, pt. 2, p. 95.
[20] *OR*, ser. 1, vol. 24, pt. 2, p. 100.

disorder. There Barton made a mistake. Seeing troops approaching through a wooded area and taking them for US soldiers, he abandoned his post and fled across Baker's Creek. In fact, it was Stephen Lee, coming to reinforce his position; but before he could get there, John Stevenson's men captured the unattended bridge.

W. L. Calhoun recalled that the 42nd was sent to hold Baker's Creek Bridge late in the afternoon. As the retreat of Pemberton's entire army got underway, they put up a fight and they themselves did not cross until everyone else was over, around midnight. "I then realized what the word tired meant…. Whatever may be said of this battle, the Confederates fought bravely for a long time, and perhaps it might have had a different result if all had been engaged at the same time and not by detachments."[21]

William Asbury Parks, chaplain of the Georgia 52nd, wrote of Champion Hill in 1899,

> The 52nd Georgia, commanded by Col. Charles Phillips of Marietta, Ga. was in the thickest of the fight, and most of his men were killed or captured. Colonel Phillips himself was —this writer remembering well with what sadness he led the Colonel's horse back to Vicksburg, for a man's horse is most intimately associated with the soldier. Capt. "Gus" Boyd of Dahlonega fell in this battle while gallantly leading his company. The commander of the 43rd Georgia, Col. "Skid" Harris, and the gallant General Lloyd Tilghman, both fell in this engagement. By a mishap not necessary to be explained, the writer found himself on the deserted battle-field after the Confederates had all fled. The Blue-coats were advancing in line but a short distance away. The only chance of escape was along a lane parallel with the advancing line. Rapid flight was the only hope. A new pair of spurs was brought into vigorous requisition.

---

[21] Calhoun, *History of the 42nd Regiment*, 32.

At least a dozen dead battery horses had to be leaped in that lane. Suddenly the lane turned at left-angles, and stretched a half-mile down towards Baker's Creek. Down this lane with race-horse speed the rider flew, while minnie-balls whizzed around too close to the ear to be musical, and raising the dust on the ground before the rider. But thanks to good fortune both rider and horse escaped.[22]

Augustus Franklin "Gus" Boyd, we recall, was the eighteen-year-old son of Colonel Wier Boyd, the original commander of the 52nd who had gone home in November and lived to have a long political career in Georgia. Brigade commander Lloyd Tilghman of Loring's Division, an engineer trained at West Point, had built forts Henry and Donelson.

News filtering back to families in Georgia took a long time, unless eyewitnesses returned home or the increasingly compromised mail system delivered personal letters. Even so, the whole picture was hard to come by. For example, in the June 30 edition of the *Southern Confederacy* newspaper of Atlanta, W. H. Vandyke, surgeon of the Georgia 43rd, published the "Official List of the Killed and Wounded at the Battle of Baker's Creek," for the 40th, 41st, 43rd, and 52nd Georgia regiments. It was tantalizingly incomplete and Vandyke cautioned that the list was "nearly correct, particularly in the list of wounded; but it is not possible to obtain a correct list of those were killed on the battlefield...." Later in the article, he appeared less confident of the facts: "I have taken all pains possible to get information as to those killed, and I am satisfied much of it may be incorrect: however, the report, imperfect as it is, may possibly relieve from painful suspense

---

[22] William Asbury Parks, "The Siege and Fall of Vicksburg, How Grant Succeeded and Pemberton Failed," *Wesleyan Christian Advocate*, March 8, 1899. Quoted in Goodson, "Part III—The Narrative," *Georgia Confederate 7,000*, 145.

some families in Georgia who may have not been able otherwise to learn the fate of their friends who went into that un-
fortunate battle." His report notes the specific location of
wounds, e.g., "Augustus Boyd, co. B, head, died on the field"
and "Capt. Wm. A Brown, co. C, both legs." He does not
mention John's brother Davis, whose military records show
that he was wounded there.[23]

In a book published in 1915, Wilbur F. Crummer of the
45th Illinois stated that after the battle ceased the wounded of
both sides were retrieved by the US forces and taken to a
house that had been turned into a hospital: "There they lay,
the blue and the gray intermingled; the same rich, young
American blood flowing out in little rivulets of crimson; each
thinking he was in the right; the one conscious of it today, the
other admitting now it were best the Union should be main-
tained one and inseparable.... The surgeons made no prefer-
ence as to which should be first treated; the blue and the gray
took their turn before the surgeon's knife."[24]

Among the Federal troops pursuing the retreating Confederates was Private Newt Gorsuch of the 16th Ohio, who
had been starved and chased out of Cumberland Gap by
Carter Stevenson's division and who had also seen his regiment shredded at Chickasaw Bayou. In his diary entry for
May 16, he tersely stated, "Hard fighting all day. Enemy routed.... Several thousand prisoners, 21 guns taken today. Follow
enemy till 10 p.m. Eat mush for supper. Sleep without cover-
ing."[25] As the retreating Rebels briefly tried to hold Black River Bridge from the evening of the sixteenth to the seventeenth,

[23] *Southern Confederacy* 3/119 (June 30, 1863): 1. Vandyke's letter was
reprinted in the July 8 issue of the *Southern Banner* newspaper of Athens,
GA.

[24] Wilbur F. Crummer, *With Grant at Fort Donelson, Shiloh and Vicksburg* (Oak Park, IL: E.C. Crummer & Co., 1915), 104.

[25] Gorsuch, *Civil War Diaries and Selected Letters*, 88.

the Ohio 16th "turned the captured guns on enemy and shelled them. Skirmish with enemy across river all eve."[26] Stevenson's division bivouacked at Bovina the night of the sixteenth and did not participate in the action at the Big Black, except that Stephen Lee's men were assigned to occupy high ground on the west bank and guard the withdrawal of the Confederate troops from the entrenchments after their defeat.[27] Before crossing the river, Barton's Brigade burned the supplies at Edwards Depot to keep them out of Federal hands.

Pemberton's order to retreat sent the surviving, uncaptured Rebels streaming back within the perimeter defenses of Vicksburg on the eighteenth, and Grant's siege began. Major Raleigh Camp of the Georgia 41st recalled that many, scattered and lost, swam the Big Black to escape.[28] Other sources state that some drowned trying to cross the river.

Once in Vicksburg, Stevenson's division "took position in the line of defense, resting its left at the railroad and its right at the redoubt on the west side of the Warrenton road. It was also held responsible for the defense of the river front for an indefinite distance between its right and the city of Vicksburg."[29] Exactly one year earlier, on May 18, 1862, David Farragut had arrived with his US naval fleet to demand that Vicksburg surrender. General M. L. Smith, Mayor Lazarus Lindsay, and the local commander, Lt. Col. James Autry, had refused.

In the fog of war, many took gallant action and many mistakes were made. Blaming goes on to this day, with Pemberton's overall lack of leadership highlighted. Questions remain. For example, why General Loring took so long to bring

---

[26] Gorsuch, *Civil War Diaries and Selected Letters*, 88.

[27] *OR*, ser. 1, vol. 24, pt. 2, p. 97.

[28] Camp, "What I Know...," 61.

[29] John S. Kountz, *Record of the Organizations Engaged in the Campaign, Siege and Defense of Vicksburg*, compiled from the Official Records (Washington, D.C.: Government Printing Office, 1901), 50.

his troops into battle remains a mystery, as does Carter Stevenson ordering the ordnance wagons of another division (Bowen's) to be moved across Baker's Creek, thus depriving Bowen's men of much-needed ammunition. For his part, Barton reported, "The heavy loss of the brigade (over 42 per cent.) is the best evidence I can give of the good behavior of the men."[30] Of his brigade, there were 58 killed, 106 wounded, and 737 captured or missing. For the division, Stevenson put the number killed at 233; wounded, 527; and captured or missing, 2,103.[31]

At Champion Hill in the space of a day, 381 Confederates had been killed, 1,018 wounded, and 2,444 captured or missing. Bowen's and Stevenson's divisions sustained the greatest losses, as the totals show. The Federals counted 310 dead, 1,844 wounded, and 187 captured or missing.[32] At the Big Black River Bridge, the US lost 39 men. Over 1,000 Rebels were captured, but the number of their casualties was not recorded. The collapse at Champion Hill would seal Vicksburg's fate.

---

[30] *OR*, ser. 1, vol. 24, pt. 2, p. 100.

[31] *OR*, ser. 1, vol. 24, pt. 2, p. 99.

[32] These numbers are not complete, as some reports were never filed.

11

River of No Return

On May 19 and 22, Grant launched two failed assaults on Vicksburg before settling down to bombard and starve the city into surrendering. Also on the nineteenth, John Douthit was again listed as ill with diarrhea. Possibly he had been ill with the same complaint—whichever disease "diarrhoea" signified—ever since it was noted on his medical record March 14. Sickness was increasing in all regiments as rations were cut and the days in the trenches, under a merciless sun, stretched out.

With the city surrounded, very few letters got out. The June 29 issue of the *Southern Confederacy* newspaper of Atlanta published a letter dated June 13 from Raleigh Camp of the 40th Georgia to his wife, which in part said:

> I learn that a man will attempt to run the blockade to-night and knowing your anxiety to hear, I gladly embrace the opportunity of sending you a letter. My health is very good and my spirits buoyant though the prospect is mingled with some doubt.
>
> It is four weeks to-day since the fight at Baker's Creek, and for 26 days we have been cut off from the outer world and closely invested, with a heavy fire on all sides.
>
> Our regiment has not suffered as much as some others, being in a less exposed position.—We have had none killed, several wounded and lost several from sickness. We

have some sickness, mostly chills, but we hope for help from Johnston soon, and can hold out longer.—Ere then we hope to be free again.[1]

In speaking for his regiment, he was of course describing the situation for the entire brigade. But by now, loved ones knew they could take only the most temporary comfort from any letter originating in Vicksburg.

There were seven entrances to the city to be guarded, six roads and the Southern Railroad line. Because Stevenson's Division had not performed well at Champion Hill, they were put in the least threatened position, back along the Warrenton road south of the city and near the railroad. Today, Confederate Avenue winds along the siege line. Still, as May wore into June, the Georgia regiments had to defend their ground vigorously. During the May 22 assault, the Warrenton Road garrison captured 107 enemy pickets. In Seth Barton's June 17 dispatch to General Stevenson, following a Federal attack that drove in his pickets, he reported,

> An effort was made last night to retake the picket posts in front of the Fortieth Georgia, but the enemy was found in so great force that the loss which must have ensued in forcing the point would have been out of proportion to the value gained. It was, therefore, abandoned, and other posts established, which, it is thought, will render the first untenable by the enemy. This proves to be the case. A dash was made on the extreme outpost of the Forty-second Georgia last night, and the post and 4 men captured. The post has been retaken this morning. An effort was also made to establish a battery opposite the Fifty-second Georgia, but was defeated.[2]

---

[1] Raleigh S. Camp, "From the 40th Georgia Regiment in Vicksburg," *Southern Confederacy* 3/118 (June 29, 1863): 1.

[2] *OR*, ser. 1, vol. 24, pt. 2, p. 342.

A week later, Stevenson reported up the chain of command, "The firing of the enemy on General Barton has been very severe to-day. They kept up a fire with nine pieces, and this evening drove in one of his pickets, capturing 7 men."[3]

Meanwhile General Johnston, settled northeast of Jackson in Canton, convinced himself that his army was "too weak" and never put it in motion to save Vicksburg. He preferred for Pemberton to break through the Federal ring and join him; but soon Pemberton's forces would be too weak physically to fight their way anywhere.

Gradually, as food and water ran out and sanitation deteriorated within the Federal cordon, a host of diseases and infections picked off more and more of the men, as did US marksmen and artillery shells. On June 25, Raleigh Camp listed the daily ration for each man: 1/4 lb. flour, 1/4 lb. bacon, 1-1/2 oz. rice, 1-1/2 oz. sugar, 1/4 lb. peas. He also mentions a "chicken pie" made of rats.[4] The story has often been told of the Federals polluting the streams that ran into Vicksburg and of the starving soldiers and citizenry turning to the meat of frogs, mules, and dogs for food.

As Pemberton played with the idea of staging a breakout, he asked his commanders about the condition of their troops. On July 2, Stevenson responded,

> ...my men are very cheerful, but from long confinement in the trenches and short rations are necessarily much enfeebled, and a considerable number would be unable to make the march and undergo the fatigues which would probably be necessary in a successful evacuation of this city. If pressed by the enemy, and it should be necessary to place the Big Black in our rear in one march, the chances are that a considerable number of those now in the trenches

---

[3] *OR*, ser. 1, vol. 24, pt. 2, pp. 342–43.

[4] Camp, "What I Know...," 77–78.

could not succeed. I believe, however, that most of them, rather than be captured, would exert themselves to the utmost to accomplish it.[5]

General Barton concurred in his July 1 response: "...I have the honor to state that probably half of them are fit to take the field. The command suffers greatly from intermittent fever, and is generally debilitated from the long exposure and inaction of the trenches. Of those now reported for duty, fully one half are undergoing treatment. These I think are unfit for the field."[6] Other officers gave similar assessments. Only Steven Lee, ever aggressive, thought his men could match up in a fight.

On July 3, an eerie quiet settled over the city after 5 p.m., when the last gun was fired in the standoff. After meeting twice with Grant to discuss terms, Pemberton surrendered the city on July 4. It was over. The men had been in the trenches forty-seven days. The Stars and Stripes replaced the Confederate flag over the courthouse. Federals and Rebels mingled like old friends and blue clads shared food with grey clads. During the siege, the US lost some 10,000 men and the Confederates upwards of 9,000.

In an account written for the Gus Boyd chapter of the United Daughters of the Confederacy in 1908, T. H. Worley of the 52nd said,

Half starved, yet we fought like heroes and we were heroes because we were fighting for a principal [sic] which was right for our homes and loved ones. I have no love for those who turned their backs on their home and went on the other side. I think they should have stayed over there. I love a true soldier even if we were foes in the strife. 4th of July 1863 we were surrendered by General Pemberton

---

[5] *OR*, ser. 1, vol. 24, pt. 2, pp. 346–47.
[6] *OR*, ser. 1, vol. 24, pt. 2, p. 347.

without rations. I had had nothing to eat for four days and the first I got was mule meat without bread.[7]

How long it took news of Vicksburg's fall to reach Martha in Fannin County, we do not know. If she read the Georgia papers, she would have received a different picture from what actually transpired. In its issue of July 21, the *Southern Recorder* of Milledgeville heaped scorn on Grant for bringing the siege to a close and allowing a dignified removal of the besieged troops. Evidently the editors would have preferred for every Confederate soldier to be killed in battle. Moreover, the paper turned around the facts to make it seem as if Pemberton were in control and the fearful Grant bowed to his wishes:

> Inasmuch as the surrender of Vicksburg was not unconditional, but the result of conference and stipulation, coupled with condition, the Atlanta *Appeal* does not think it can be regarded by the enemy as a complete and victorious triumph. At least it does not carry with it that prestige which an unconditional conquest by assault would have given it. It bears a strong resemblance to the capture of Monterey by General Taylor, which was robbed of much of its glory by permitting *Ampudia* and his troops to march out with their arms and banners flying. It is true that we lose the position, together with our ordnance stores, and whatever of public property there may be in the city, but the spirit and *morale* of our army are preserved. The courage of our soldiers has not been subdued nor will they feel the humiliation they would otherwise have experienced, had they been conquered at the cannon's mouth and forced to lay down their arms unconditionally. The starving out of a garrison may be a conquest of the locality, but it certainly cannot be regarded as a defeat or conquest of the soldiery.

---

[7] Document in possession of Randy Woolley, who posted it on the Civil War Message Board at www.history-sites.com.

The acceptance by Grant of the terms proposed, shows that he felt himself in a precarious position, and was ready to meet Pemberton on half-way ground. He was not unaware of the éclat which was unconditional surrender of the place would have given to the victory, and he would most certainly never have acceded to Pemberton's terms, and permitted him and his officers to march out with their side arms, regimental colors, horses, and other private property, had he been sure of his own safety and confident of his ability to conquer the place by force of arms.[8]

Soon Martha would have heard that the 29,000-plus troops had been paroled, not imprisoned. The 52nd was given a thirty-day furlough and men were arriving home. At last John would see his beloved family and be able to speak with "inquiring friends."

Weeks went by. Neither John nor Davis was seen or heard from. The last letter Martha received from John had been written May 6. Other families whose sons had been in the siege began receiving letters again, as regiments re-formed. Martha's granddaughter and Victoria's daughter, Essie Jane Cochran, later remembered that when John's letters stopped coming, Martha and a sister-in-law rode horseback as far as McMinn County, Tennessee, to try to find out what happened to him; but they learned little.

Nearly three months after the surrender, Benjamin M. Tilley, a neighbor of the Douthits and a member of the 52nd, sat down to respond to a letter he had received from Martha.

---

[8] *Southern Recorder* 44/29 (July 21, 1863): 3. The article appears to be reprinted from another paper, perhaps the *Memphis Daily Appeal*. Sometimes dubbed "the Moving Appeal" because the newspaper kept changing locations to keep away from Union troops, it was then being published in Atlanta.

Fannin Co. Sept the 29th 1863

Mrs. Martha E. Douthite yours of the 19th was received the 26th. I have not saw Mr. Douthite since about the 20th of July; I went and saw him he was on a boat and started home that eavenig; by the way of New Orleans. W.D. Douthite[9] was with him; but very unwell; J. M.--- thought he was on the mend; but I think he was about like he was the 10th, he was in good heart of gitting home [illegible]

I cannot see why it is that Davis did not write if he reached the confederate lines; some accident must have occurred for he was a waiting on John; and able to go where he pleased.

If the boys died in Federaldom you may be well assured that they were well cared for; if they are not dead they are in the Hospital at Mobile on this side but they would have wrote it seems like the Federals would alow any to step the other side of Mo after starting

--this is all I can tell about the Boys as I remaned at Vicksburg until the 30th of July; A.D.

yours respectively B. M. Tilley

I was left there to wait on four of our Co to wit W.F. Bulliard J-P. Free S.P. Bradley and G. W. Marshall. Marshall only lived to get home

(W.F. Bulliard died at Vicksburg the 28th of July 1863) I have rote this for the boys of Capt. Browns Co to see if they are not gone back I have been sick ever since I come home and am just able to set up to rite this with chills and Fever.

B.M. Tilley

It took days to obtain the signatures of the defeated army on the individual forms of surrender. On July 15, both John

---

[9] Warren Davis Douthit, John's brother. Also referred to as Davis in Tilley's letter.

and Davis gave their word (parole) that they would "not take up arms against the United States, nor serve in any military police, or constabulary force in any Fort, Garrison, field work, held by the Confederate States of America, against the United States of America, nor a guard of any prisons, depots or stores nor discharge any duties usually performed by Officers or soldiers against the United States of America, until duly exchanged by the proper authorities."[10] Their signatures were witnessed by Captain George W. Goddard of the Ohio 31st Infantry.

They were free to go. But both signed while in Vicksburg's Washington Hospital, which before the siege was the Washington Hotel, which one earlier visitor likened to "an old London tavern."[11] Located at Washington and China streets, the building was the largest in a block of buildings that the needs of war had turned into a medical complex. It commanded a view of the river below. William Lovelace Foster, chaplain of the 35th Mississippi Infantry, recalled, "[Washington Hospital] was comparatively secure from those troublesome mortar shells—for the most of them passed over & it was too far from our lines to be disturbed by firing from that direction....This hospital contained the sick from the whole army....Dr. W[hitfield] with several assistants attended to the invalids. All the rooms were soon crowded with the sick & dying—Some in bunks and some upon the floor. Everything was conducted as well as possible but O the horrors of a hospital!"[12] How long the brothers were treated there is not known. No Vicksburg hospital records from the war survive.

---

[10] Standard parole document, John M. Douthit, Confederate Service Records, National Archives.

[11] Walker, *Vicksburg: A People at War*, 10.

[12] William Lovelace Foster, *Vicksburg: Southern City under Siege* (New Orleans: The Historic New Orleans Collection, 1995), 45.

The day after they signed their parole papers, John and Davis, too ill to be released, were put on a hospital ship, the *H. Chouteau*, along with some 600 Confederate prisoners of war in similar condition. The destination was the military hospitals at Mobile Bay. Tilley indicates that Davis was in better health, looking after John and perhaps able to start home and/or to write. Tilley's positive opinion of "Federal-dom" provides a clue to his shifting allegiances. He would desert the Confederate Army and in 1864 sign up with the 10th Tennessee Cavalry, US Army, serving with them until the end of the war. Of the fellow soldiers mentioned by Tilley, Samuel P. Bradley of Company H, who enlisted with John at Morganton, was eventually "delivered off Mobile Harbor" from a hospital ship, presumably to the hospital. Returned to the Confederacy in a prisoner exchange, he died in an Atlanta hospital on August 4.[13] John P. Free, who also was paroled in hospital, died in Vicksburg of "chronic diarrhoea"[14] and is buried there in Cedar Hill Cemetery.

However, Benjamin Tilley would not have seen John and Davis on July 20. On that date, the brothers were taken off the *H. Chouteau* at New Orleans and were admitted to the St. Louis Hospital, heretofore the elegant St. Louis Hotel, which had a slave auction block in its rotunda. It may be that Davis was well enough to go on but did not want to leave John. John, patient number 508, died July 21 or 23 of "chronic diarrhoea." July 21 was his twenty-sixth birthday. A handwritten note on his record says, "entered into dead book." He was buried in Cypress Grove Cemetery Number 2. A month later, on August 22, Davis, patient 504, died and was buried in Cypress Grove #2 as well.

---

[13] Samuel P. Bradley, Confederate Service records, National Archives.
[14] John P. Free, Confederate Service Record, National Archives.

In Martha's lifetime, the family never knew the exact resting place of John and Davis. Two generations later, Essie Jane Cochran wrote in an unpublished family sketch, "It was thought that he died and was buried somewhere around New Orleans or Vicksburg, Mississippi. Someday I want to go to the National cemetery at Vicksburg and try to find his grave and marker."

If the family had access to *The Confederate Union* newspaper of Milledgeville, Georgia, they would have seen this notice in the November 24, 1863, issue, under the heading *Georgia and Alabama Prisoners at St. Louis Hospital*: "The Mobile Advertiser and Register publishes the following list of prisoners who had died or been transferred from the St. Louis Hospital in New Orleans. It is said to have been the dying request of many of them that their families should be informed of their fate." There followed a list of twenty-five names, including "J.M. Douthier [sic]," who died on July 21, and W. D. Douthit, who died on August 22.[15]

On All Souls' Day (November 1) in 1863, a fourteen-year-old New Orleans girl visited Cypress Grove #2 and wrote a letter to a relative, describing the Confederate graves. The relative passed the letter on to an interested party and eventually excerpts were published in the December 24 issue of the *Memphis Daily Appeal*. Because of this young correspondent, we can know more about the resting place of John and Davis than Martha and her daughters ever knew:

> The Confederate graves were beautifully decorated, not one neglected. They presented a glorious contrast to the graves of the Federals, some of which were covered with

---

[15] *The Confederate Union* (Milledgeville, GA) 24/27 (November 24, 1863): 3. In regimental records, John's date of death is often listed as August 16, the day Martha used in her application for a widow's pension after the war. Clearly this is incorrect.

weeds that made it almost impossible to see the head-boards. Where the Union ladies were we should like to know. In the center of the Confederate burial ground (which is in Cypress Grove) there is a cross about seven feet high, covered with black velvet and spangled with gold. In golden letters inscribed on the front of the cross, are these words, "To our Southern brothers, by the ladies of New Orleans." On the other side, on the cross piece, are three wreaths, the one on each end being red, and the one in the center white—which gives the red, white and red of our flag—while the top of the cross is surmounted with a wreath of olive. The name, regiment, and place of death is inscribed on each head-board. There was not a blade of grass an inch high to be seen about them. Each head-board is entwined with a wreath of evergreen, inter-spersed with white flowers, ...emblems of the hearts of our dead heroes, while the graves themselves were planted with red and white flowers....[16]

She appends a list of the inscribed names, grouped by state. Evidently the head-boards, or some other signage, told the hospitals at which some of the soldiers died. Among the dead from Louisiana, Georgia, Alabama, and Arkansas are twelve members of Barton's Brigade and eighteen from other Georgia regiments. "J. W. Dawther" and "W. E. Douther" appear as two of three dead from the 52nd, the former grouped with those dying July 25 and the latter with those dying August 23. This would not be the last time their names were misspelled and their death dates recorded incorrectly. Perhaps it was not even their final resting place.

---

[16] *Memphis Daily Appeal* 14/269 (December 24, 1863): 2.

12

Going On

In fall 1863, Barton's Brigade re-formed and fought on under the command of General Marcellus Augustus Stovall. Today it is known as the Barton-Stovall Brigade. General Barton was transferred to the Virginia theater, where eventually he was removed from his command twice for insubordination but was reinstated each time.

The numbers of the brigade had dwindled; many had died. Also, not every soldier went back after the furlough following Vicksburg. In September, after Chickamauga, desertions increased. In the December 30 issue of the *Southern Watchman* newspaper of Decatur, Georgia, Captain Rufus Asbury offered a $30 reward for deserters from the 52nd and listed sixty-five names.[1]

In October, Davis Douthit's first child, a daughter named for his mother, was born. On January 11, 1864, the wills of John and Davis were probated. In August 1864, two weeks after the Battle of Atlanta, Alfred Weaver, John's and Davis's cousin-in-law, wrote to Confederate headquarters:

Camp 52d Ga Regt.
Near Atlanta Ga. Aug. 4, 1864
S. Cooper A. & I.G. [Adjutant and Inspector General]
    Richmond Va.

---

[1] *Southern Watchman* 10/40 (December 30, 1863): 2.

I have the honor to tender my Resignation on the following grounds to wit: There are only three men present in my Company for duty and only Seven on my "Muster Rolls" and I have no prospect of recruiting it, and there are three officers belonging to my company. I therefore am anxious to Join Some other command.

I have the honor to be Your Obt. Servant

Alfred Weaver
2nd Lt. Co. H 52nd Ga. Regt.

I certify on honor that I do am not in possession of any property belonging to the Confederate states, That I am not indebted to the Confederate states on any account whatever, That I have never been absent from my command without leave, and that there are no charges preferred against me which can affect my pay.

Alfred Weaver
2nd Lt. Co "h"52 Ga. Regt.[2]

Weaver's resignation was passed up the line to General John Bell Hood, who accepted it, provided that another post might be found for Weaver. The resignation became effective August 31. There is no further record of Weaver's service. By March 1865, at the Battle of Bentonville in North Carolina, the entire Barton-Stovall Brigade numbered around 400 officers and enlisted men, down from the approximately 7,000 men enrolled.

A few days after Alfred Weaver wrote his letter, and a year after John and Davis died, John Vandiver Willson, Martha's oldest brother, wrote a different kind of letter. Cumberland Gap was again under US control and Willson was stationed there with the 11th Tennessee Cavalry USA, which he had joined in September 1863. Willson was married and had

---

[2] Alfred Weaver, Confederate Service Records, National Archives.

named his first child (born 1854) Martha Emmeline for his oldest sister. His letter demonstrates how little Martha and Davis's wife Harriet knew of the brothers' fates. Instead of the St. Louis hospital in New Orleans, John Willson appears to have been under the impression that the men died at Orleans hospital in St. Louis, Missouri. Such a hospital did not exist.

> Cumberland Gap Tenn.
> Aug. 8, 1864
> Carridg(?) Officer of Orleans Hospittle Saint Louis
> I have the honor to address your magesty through request of two Rebel prisenors wives who died at Saint Luis. If you are known to their Death will you be sou kind as to give me the date of their Death & also whether they maid any professions before departing this life. It was for the love I have for my sisters that I write to for this information & not that I love those who died. Their names are John Douthit & Davis Douthit.
> Give me the above information if will to oblige your obt. Servt.
>
> John V. Wilson [sic] Private
> Co (G.) 11th Tenn. U.S. Cav.[3]

The letter made its way to St. Louis, Missouri, where several notations were added on the back. Dr. M. D. Mills, an army medical director, referred the letter to the surgeon in charge of Gratiot Street Prison Hospital. There it arrived August 16. Mills added the note, "Wishes information of the Death of Davis & Joseph/John Douthit, Confederate prisoners whether they made any profession before their death." On August 18, a surgeon named G. M. Youngblood "respectfully" returned the letter to Dr. Mills, explaining that his hospital

---

[3] John Vandiver Willson letter, Civil War Miscellaneous documents, National Archives.

records did not show either a David or a Joseph Douthit to have been patients. Dr. Mills then referred the letter to the Provost Marshall's office. There, someone wrote on the back that a Corporal John Douthit of Longstalk's (?) Battery C.S.A was sent to Camp (illegible) on August 13. "No word of any other Douthit except a female of that name." This was a Missouri woman, Nannie Douthit, who was being held in Gratiot Street Prison. In fact, Corporal John Douthit was someone else, from another state.

John Willson's lack of affection for his brothers-in-law suggests either that the family was typical of so many in Fannin County—split over the war—or that he wanted to assure his superiors that his interest in two dead Rebels did not affect his loyalty to the Union. Or perhaps both. Willson was looking for assurances that the brothers had died a Good Death, not a Bad Death. Never in the history of the country had so many people died away from home, with no loved ones to witness their last hours and ascertain their states of mind regarding religion and salvation. Drew Gilpin Faust observes, "The concept of the Good Death was central to mid-nineteenth century America, as it had long been at the core of Christian practice. Dying was an art, and the tradition of *ars moriendi* had provided rules of conduct for the moribund and their attendants since at least the fifteenth century: how to give up one's soul 'gladlye and wilfully'; how to meet the devil's temptations of unbelief, despair, impatience, and worldly attachment; how to pattern one's dying on that of Christ; how to pray."[4] One's mental state, or even facial expression, at the moment of death, could provide a clue as to whether or not the dying soldier would be received into heaven. So it was incumbent on those who witnessed the deaths of soldiers to take

---

[4] Drew Gilpin Faust, *This Republic of Suffering: Death and the American Civil War* (New York: Vintage Civil War Library, 2009), 6.

note of last words, or whether the eyes were turned upwards, and other such indications of dying "right with God." Fellow soldiers, doctors, nurses, and other witnesses wrote to families when possible and shared details of the final state of loved ones. Faust states that witnesses were by and large honest, relaying, if necessary, details of a Bad Death, in which, for example, the dying man cursed God or refused to pray. But at the same time, they struggled to hold on to the old, comforting patterns that made sense of slaughter, as did those at home. "Narratives of dying well may have served as a kind of lifeline between the new world of battle and the old world at home."[5]

But in this regard, as in so much else, John Douthit remains an indistinct figure. His letters speak of hearing sermons in camp, but he never mentions God, faith, salvation, or facing death. The nearest he comes to any of it is to assure Martha that "I am still alive" in letters from Tennessee and Mississippi. His personal remarks are centered on a longing for home. Martha herself was a devout Methodist all her life. Her father had been a circuit-riding Methodist preacher. John had several uncles who were Methodist preachers. But he never wrote of religion or asked the Big Questions in his correspondence. Neither did he speak of fighting for a noble cause, another path to the Good Death. Martha and her family had to go on without the consolation of knowing about the last moments of John and his brother, though presumably she received other information about their time in the military from returning soldiers. The 52nd was in the army surrendered by Joseph E. Johnston at the end of the war in April 1865.

Today, in regimental lists, John Douthit's death date is recorded erroneously as August 16, the date Martha used in her 1910 pension application. Davis's name appears neither on

---

[5] Faust, *This Republic of Suffering*, 31.

the regimental rolls nor on the war memorial in Fannin County.

In April 1867, the *Times-Picayune* newspaper of New Orleans reported that the bodies of Federal soldiers in Cypress Grove Cemetery #2 were being exhumed and moved to the National Cemetery "on the battle field of Chalmette." There followed a description of the graves of "upwards of five thousand soldiers" buried in that cemetery, which would have pertained both to Union and Confederates:

> At the time of interment, the bodies were placed in plain pine or cypress coffins, and buried only about a foot and a half or two below the surface of the soil, and even at those depths, had to be sunk in water; there, in those watery graves, have they laid ever since. We noticed that many of the coffins had become entirely rotten, while only portions of some were decayed. The most of them, however, were in a sound condition. We saw several lying open, and there revealed the ghastly skeletons of what were once human beings, walking the earth in all the pride and vigor of manhood....[6]

In the January 5, 1869, *Times-Picayune*, it was reported that the Ladies' Benevolent Association was hosting a benefit to "complete the tomb in which are being placed the Confederate dead in this city. Circumstances...have rendered it necessary to remove the bodies from their first resting place, Cypress Grove Cemetery No. 2, where they were interred over a wide surface, now required for avenues, walks and grading purposes. ...up to this time no action has been taken...to remove the remains of the Confederate dead for more perfect and satisfactory protection."[7] In 1873, some six hundred re-

---

[6] "Wednesday Afternoon Edition," *The Times-Picayune* (New Orleans), April 24, 1867, p. 1. No volume or number.

[7] *The Times-Picayune*, 32/ 291 (January 5, 1869): 3.

mains of Confederate soldiers were finally moved to a mass grave in Greenwood Cemetery, where a large Confederate monument was dedicated in 1874. It is presently unknown whether John and Davis were moved to Greenwood, there being more soldiers' graves at Cypress Grove No. 2 than the six hundred that were moved. In 1986, when Canal Boulevard was again extended, human remains and wooden coffins were discovered where the cemetery had been located; 157 anonymous burials were recovered.[8]

Besides all the uncertainties surrounding soldiers' fates, the civilian population in north Georgia suffered ever more daily privations and insults as the war went on. Impressment laws allowed the Confederate government to seize private property as needed. Resentment rose against a government that was nominally in favor of states' rights while exercising ever more centralized control. Union sympathizers were also commandeering horses and goods. As a result of these conditions, more soldiers deserted, despite the peril of doing so, and came home to protect their families. From the beginning of the conflict, they had wanted to serve closer to home, anyway. The anger against government intrusion in north Georgia moved Governor Brown to send troops to quell dissent, thus increasing government intervention in daily lives. Further, political corruption affected food distribution to a starving populace: "Enraged citizens from Fannin County called on the governor to remove their inferior court justices 'for want of energy incapacity, [and] misapplication of the public fund corn.'"[9]

---

[8] Cypress Grove Cemetery No. 2, a potters' field, was also known as Charity Hospital Cemetery No. 2. It was the resting place of poor people, hospital charity cases, "enslaved people, immigrants, victims of a yellow fever epidemic, and fallen Civil War soldiers" (Ethan Ranck, "Cypress Grove II Cemetery," edited by D. Ryan Gray and Charlotte Wilcox, at https://neworleanshistorical.org/items/show/1253).

[9] Williams et al., *Plain Folk in a Rich Man's War*, 66.

To go back a few months, in January 1863, Colonel George W. Lee arrived in Dahlonega with troops to keep order and to round up deserters and dissenters. "Within a week," writes Jonathan Sarris, "Lee's expedition had forced over one thousand deserters and draft dodgers into the Confederate army. Fifty-three people were sent back to Atlanta for trial on charges ranging from 'aiding and abetting treason' to being a 'citizen in arms.'"[10] Hostility among citizens increased. Even pro-Confederate citizens asked that Lee and his men be replaced by locals. In February a large anti-Confederate meeting was held at Hot House, where the Douthits lived. Many dissenters were not so much pro-Union as they were anti-government-of-any-kind. Increasingly, families petitioned the governor for exemptions to military service so that essential work could be done. In many families, women and children worked in the fields, there being no one else to do it. Despite warnings not to worry the soldiers, some families pressured loved ones to come home and hide out. With each passing day, life grew harder and more dangerous for both sides in Fannin County. Essential goods, such as salt and paper, became scarce. Drought ravaged the crops. Family allegiances were split and neighbors grew mistrustful of each other.

A few stories of the home front have been passed down through the Douthit-Willson family. By now the details are faint and worn, like the features of faces on old coins. Essie Cochran, granddaughter of John and Martha, wrote in unpublished family recollections many years later of the time the Yankees came to the Willson farm and stole the livestock. Martha's little mare Sparky was one of the horses stolen, so the event probably happened after she and her two children moved back to live with her parents in John's absence. That night there was a full moon. Martha and her father followed

---

[10] Sarris, *A Separate Civil War*, 91.

the trail of the thieves and found their livestock herded into a clearing in the woods. Softly Martha called the mare's name and the horse came to her. She and her father hurried away, taking Sparky with them. What sort of "Yankees" these were is unknown—Soldiers? Tories? Common thieves? All were active in Fannin Couny, as were Confederate operatives who took from the general population what was needed for the war effort.

At least two members of Martha's immediate family left the area because of the lawlessness in Fannin County. Her older brother Richard, a merchant, moved to Athens, Tennessee, and stayed until the war was over. In 1863, as noted, her brother John Vandiver Willson "refugeed" to Kentucky and joined the 11th Tennessee Cavalry, a Union regiment being assembled at Camp Nelson. Sometime after that, neighbor Richard Curtis (and soon-to-be in-law) and his brother John were walking along a road in Fannin County when a Captain Elisha Green of the Home Guard, bent on rounding up slackers and deserters for the Rebel army, ordered them to halt. When they ran instead, he opened fire. The two men escaped unharmed but were so angered by Green's action that they, their brothers Tom and William, and some friends all fled into Union territory. The Curtises joined the Federal Quartermaster's Department in Kentucky.[11]

Henry Clay Curtis, son of Richard Curtis and nephew of John and Martha, took down another family story his mother Julitty (or Condecy, as John calls his sister-in-law in his letters) told him when she was an old woman. Richard Curtis and Julitty were sweethearts. They married on October 20, 1864, at the Willson home in Fannin County and then Rich-

---

[11] Kathleen M. Thompson, ed., *Touching Home: A Collection of History and Folklore from the Copper Basin, Fannin County Area* (Orlando, FL: Daniels Publishers, 1976), 113.

ard fled to Tennessee. Some months later, missing her husband, Julitty decided to make the dangerous journey to Athens to see him. She was accompanied by a neighbor, Margaret Stuart, whose husband Iley was also in Tennessee, serving in a Union regiment. As the story goes, the two women took the Old Copper Road along the Ocoee River. Today US Highway 64, this road snaked through "wild and rugged" territory populated by panthers, bears, and wildcats. Even more dangerous, however, were the bushwhackers and robbers who preyed on travelers and on wagons carrying copper ore from the mines in the Copper Basin to the railroad at Cleveland, Tennessee, and returning with payrolls. Having only one horse, the women took turns riding it and traveled at night a "treacherous 18 miles" through the mountains. They had to be particularly quiet going past the Halfway House, a notorious tavern where thieves congregated. Fortunately, the tavern was dark and they met no one on their journey. Richard and Julitty lived on a farm near Athens for a year and a half until order was restored in Fannin County.

This story has been published and republished, but there is a problem with the timing. If Julitty waited months to join Richard in Tennessee, she could not have made the trip with Margaret Stuart. In fall 1864, Iley Stuart and Solomon Stansbury, a neighbor of the Douthits on Hot House Creek, rode into Fannin County from Tennessee with a group of soldiers under the command of William Twiggs of the 5th Tennessee Mounted Infantry, a Union regiment. Twiggs, of Stock Hill, had served in the 52nd Georgia with John Douthit before changing sides. The purpose of their incursion has been variously described. Unionists later said Twiggs was on a legitimate recruiting trip for the army. He himself was supposed to have vowed to "drive the Rebels out" of north Georgia. In Dahlonega, Colonel James Findley, once also in the 52nd but now an officer in the Home Guard, heard that Twiggs was stealing horses and raiding the homes of Confederate families. He sent a group of militiamen under Captain Francis Marion Williams after the group.

On October 20, the day of Richard and Julitty's marriage, when Stuart and some others stopped at Vanzant's store to shoe some horses and mules they had taken, the militia caught them. Stansbury was on picket and was captured as well. The group was taken to the Dahlonega jail twenty miles away. However, Twiggs and some recruits escaped back into Tennessee.

Colonel Findley did not believe the prisoners deserved a trial. He considered them to be Tory outlaws and not part of the US Army, though at least some were wearing Federal uniforms. Perhaps he was particularly irked that seventeen members of the Union guerrilla unit he was pursuing had served in the Georgia 52nd before switching sides.[12] He therefore ordered Iley Stuart, Solomon Stansbury, and a recruit named William Witt to be shot. On October 22 a detachment under William R. Crisson took them to Bearden's Bridge Hill, where a seven-man firing squad dispatched them. An 1877 affidavit filed by Stuart's widow Margaret as part of an application to receive a US army pension for his service, states, "[Margaret Stuart] gets the date he was captured by the rebels from this circumstance a neighbor girl was married the day he was captured on 20 of October 1864, and he was killed on October 22, 1864 at Delonaga [sic], Georgia."[13] She would have been referring to the marriage of Richard Curtis and Julietta Condecy "Juilitty" Willson. Incidentally, also on October 20, John's first cousin, forty-five-year-old Lorenzo Maxefield

---

[12] Robert S. Davis, Jr. and William Kinsland, "Forgotten Union Guerillas of the North Georgia Mountains," *North Georgia Journal* 5/2 (summer 1988): 30–49.

[13] Iley Stuart, US Army pension files, National Archives.

Douthit, joined the 5th Tennessee Mounted Infantry of the Union Army in Cleveland, Tennessee. Lorenzo's son Davis had joined the same regiment in August.

After the war, both Mary Stansbury and Margaret Stuart, widows of Solomon and Iley respectively, applied for pensions on the grounds that their husbands were killed while on government business. William A. Twiggs, who had moved to Arkansas, deposed that on May 18, 1869, "…Stuart volunteered in the service of the United States on or about September 25, 1864, and that he served temporarily in Company H Fifth Tennessee Mounted Infantry, to repel rebel raids in Fannin County, Georgia, and that while on picket in the regular line of duty October 20, 1864, he was captured and killed by the rebels who made a raid on the picket post."[14] To help the widow's cause, William R. Crisson admitted under oath in 1869 that he shot Stuart. Richard Curtis attested to his acquaintance with Stuart and his knowledge of Stuart's death. Mary A. Willson, Martha Douthit's mother and John's mother-in-law, filed an affidavit describing a twenty-year acquaintance with the Stuarts and giving the birthdates of their minor children, for whom aid was being sought. That the Willsons stood by their Union neighbors attests to their broad sympathies during the war.

Like the rest of the country, Fannin was counting its dead and trying to heal. This was not easy. Regarding north Georgia, I. W. Avery noted in his 1881 history of the war period, "It was a suggestive coincidence that this section of Georgia, the most reluctant in going into secession, was the most sorely punished by the resulting war."[15] Bad feelings lingered. For example, Thomas R. Trammell, the census taker of 1860 with whom we began our story, returned from service with the

---

[14] Stuart pension files.

[15] Avery, *History of the State of Georgia from 1850 to 1881*, 339.

Georgia 11th Infantry and made it his business to expose some citizens who pretended to have fought on the winning side.

The 1870 census found Martha living with her two daughters near Morganton in Fannin County.[16] John's aunt Levisa and husband William Galloway were also living in Morganton, in the household of their son. Harriet Garren Douthit, Davis's wife, had remarried in 1868.

Besides those mentioned so far, many other friends and relatives were no more. For example, Martha's first cousin Julius, son of her Uncle Levi Willson, had perished in the Battle of Chattanooga. But life continued and as the 1870s proceeded, the family celebrated several weddings and funerals. John's brother Solomon, the teacher, married Amanda Howard in 1872. Levisa Galloway, sister of John's mother, died in 1873. Columbus Weaver, son of Alfred Weaver of the 52nd and Margaret Douthit Weaver, married John Douthit's youngest sister, Rebeckah in 1874. Julitty, the daughter John left to go off to war and who was named for Martha's sister, married Joseph Willis in January 1877; and daughter Victoria, whom he never got to see, married Joseph Elisha Cochran in January 1880. Joseph was named for Joseph Elisha Brown, Georgia's Civil War governor. His uncle, Nathan Matteson Cochran, had served briefly as a second lieutenant in company G of the 52nd. Nathan was sent home from Camp Van Dorn in Knoxville in June 1862. A doctor N. F. Howard declared him incapable of performing "a soldier's duty in the field" due to "dyspepsia and rheumatism of the kidneys." In a note on the back of the letter, Colonel Phillips concurred, saying that Cochran was "not physically or mentally able to discharge duties."[17] Nathan Cochran died in 1917.

---

[16] The wrong name is given for one daughter.

[17] Nathan M. Cochran, Confederate Service Records, National Archives.

On July 10, 1879, Martha married Thomas Farmer Anderson (1822–1880), a widower who lived nearby. As a blacksmith, Anderson was exempted from military service. But in an affidavit signed February 8, 1877, in support of Mary Stansbury's pension application, Thomas Anderson declared that he was part of Captain William Twiggs's group of Union sympathizers or soldiers who were captured at Vanzant's store by Colonel James Findley's forces. He, however, escaped at Gaddistown the night of their capture, before Iley Stuart, Solomon Stansbury, and William Witt were taken to Bearden's Bridge Hill and shot.[18] The Anderson and Willson families intermarried further. Levi's daughter Urania, for example, married Thomas Anderson's son John, who had served in three years in the US Army.

But Martha was not to enjoy this marriage, either, for long. In 1880, a typhoid epidemic swept Fannin County. Thomas died intestate on July 23, almost seven years to the day after John Douthit passed away of typhoid in New Orleans. Anderson's daughter Laura had died in May and daughter Sarah in June. Martha petitioned the court for one year's support from her second husband's estate and received one hundred dollars.

In 1882, under contract to write *Life on the Mississippi*, Mark Twain traveled by steamboat down the Mississippi River for the first time since the Civil War. In New Orleans he stopped at various places he had known in his youth, including the St. Louis Hotel, the building in which John and Davis Douthit died when it was a Civil War hospital. "We visited the old St. Louis Hotel, now occupied by municipal offices," wrote Twain in his subsequent book. "There is nothing strikingly remarkable about it; but one can say of it as of the Acad-

---

[18] Fannin County Court Records. Transcribed by Special Agent John Wager.

emy of Music in New York, that if a broom or a shovel has ever been used in it there is no circumstantial evidence to back up the fact."[19] The war years had not been kind to the building; and one assumes Twain did not know how many sick and wounded had passed through its doors, and how many died there.

Martha Willson Douthit Anderson never married again. In later life, she split her time between her two daughters' households. Martha's great-granddaughter and this writer's mother, Rubye Cochran Fowler, remembered that Martha was called "Little Grandma" in the family because she was so much smaller than her daughter Victoria. She commanded respect because she demanded it and because she received a widow's pension for John's service. In 1885, she gave land for the Sugar Creek Methodist Church to be built on. Also, she could buy small luxuries, such as brown sugar, because she had cash. Rubye wrote in an undated, unpublished family sketch,

> She kept the sugar in a tin bucket hanging on a nail above her bed. Once a day, she would share it with the grand-children present. "Hold out your hand," she demanded.... My brother would hold out both hands, and she would give him an extra portion—the son she had been deprived of because of war. Little Grandma's kindness and generosity were well known in the family and community, but stories of her temper and spunk are documented in family letters....[She] carried her own weight in my father's family with such tasks as peeling apples, stringing beans, rocking babies, knitting socks and mittens, mending work clothes and occasionally adding fuel to the wood-burning cook stove and fire place....As the queen bee in the big family Little Grandma passed along her skills in food preservation to all who entered the hive. There were ap-

---

[19] Mark Twain, *Life on the Mississippi* (New York: Penguin Books, 1986), 314.

ples to dry; hominy and kraut to make; cucumbers, corn and beans to pickle; bacon, hams and sausage to cure; and seeds to save for next year's planting.

Rubye Fowler remembered that one Christmas, when all the family was expected to be present for Christmas dinner at the home of Joseph and Victoria Cochran, Little Grandma became worried that there would not be enough meat for the meal. While she was in her room making her bed, the women assembled seven grandchildren and gave each a platter of meat to parade around Little Grandma's room while all sang "Bringing in the Sheaves." They carried pork, beef, chicken, duck, rabbit, squirrel, and quail. The Cochrans were known as "good livers," which among other things meant they set a fine table.

As Martha aged, she became deaf, or so the family believed. Rubye recalled that one autumn, her grandmother Victoria Douthit Cochran put rounds of pumpkin near the hearth to dry, much as the Cherokee had done. In the winter, the dried pumpkin slices would be reconstituted with water to make pies. Rubye and her sister Bonnie were told to watch the pumpkin and keep it from burning. Because they wanted to go out and play, they pushed the pumpkin rings closer to the fire. Each time they did so, Little Grandma, who lived in a back bedroom of the Cochran farmhouse on Sugar Creek, would appear and pull the pumpkin back. Believing her to be deaf, Bonnie exclaimed to Rubye, "I wish that old heifer would leave the pumpkin alone," and Rubye laughed. Whereupon Little Grandma whipped a wooden cooking spoon out of her apron pocket and cracked her two great-granddaughters on their skulls. She was known to declare that she would chop the fingers off of any child who bothered her while she was cooking; but she would also give them Confederate paper money as keepsakes. She died at her daughter Julitty's house in 1927 at age ninety, having outlived all her siblings. For years, in the box that held John's letters, she also kept a black dress to be buried in.

Afterword

Tragedy and the Common Man

As one thinks of the two brief, nearly unknown lives of John M. and Warren Davis Douthit, expended in a lost cause, the word *tragic* leaps to mind. But were the lives of John and Davis tragic? What does tragic mean in the context of this war? Many events today are labeled tragic, and the term "senseless tragedy" is applied to all manner of occurrences in which unwitting or innocent people are killed by fire, flood, storms, car wrecks, gun accidents, plane crashes. But historically, the tragic death is, by definition, a meaningful death, not a "senseless" one.

Certainly, there is a kind of noble stoicism about these men. John and Davis did not seek either combat or glory. It is doubtful that when they mustered in, they could have conceived of the horrors and hardships they would face; the acts they would commit; or the suffering they would witness, inflict, and undergo. By Aristotle's definition, they were not tragic heroes, being neither high-born nor better than the average man. But their story does evoke pity and fear, as was the aim of classical Greek tragedy. We feel pity for them and their families, and we fear that some other war could force us into similar situations. At the end of their story, the reader may experience what classical tragedy provided: a catharsis, or release of emotion.

Writing in 1949, Arthur Miller noted that few tragedies are written anymore, perhaps because nowadays people are seen to be "below tragedy," that is, unworthy of the designation. However, Miller believed "that the common man is as apt a subject for tragedy in its highest sense as kings were.... I think the tragic feeling is evoked in us when we are in the presence of a character who is ready to lay down his life, if need be, to secure one thing—his sense of personal dignity."[1] Here we are reminded of John's statement that, despite his desperate wish to see Martha and the girls, he would not desert his post. Miller, of course, is speaking about plays and how to construct them. But he is also talking about the way the world works, and so his remarks can be applied to what his plays are based on—real life. Miller continues, "From Orestes to Hamlet, Medea to Macbeth, the underlying struggle [is that of] the individual attempting to gain his 'rightful' position in his society. Sometimes he is one who has been displaced from it, sometimes one who seeks to attain it for the first time, but the fateful wound from which the inevitable events spiral is the wound of indignity, and its dominant force is indignation. Tragedy, then, is the consequence of a man's total compulsion to evaluate himself justly."

Whatever one thinks of the causes of the Civil War or of the Southern position, we know that the right to self-determination was paramount to many Southerners or became so. John and Davis were common men, of no wealth, status, or even military standing. Miller says, "Insistence upon the rank of the tragic hero, or the so-called nobility of his character is really but a clinging to the outward forms of tragedy....The quality in such plays that does shake us...derives from the underlying fear of being displaced, the disaster inherent in being torn away from our chosen image of what or who we are in

---

[1] Arthur Miller, "Tragedy and the Common Man," February 27, 1949, *New York Times*, at http://movies2.nytimes.com/books/00/11/12/specials/miller-common.html, unpaged.

this world....it is the common man who knows this fear best." Moreover, "the thrust for freedom is the quality in tragedy which exalts....The commonest of men may take on that stature to the extent of his willingness to throw all he has into the contest, the battle to secure his rightful place in the world."

As far as we know, John and Davis Douthit, unlike the soldiers of James McPherson's research, never said what they were fighting for or declared for a side except through their actions, which of course speak volumes. The rhetoric of the time suggests that the Douthit brothers would have believed they were fighting for freedom, fighting for the social identity and dignity of themselves and their families, as they conceived it. Because they were willing to risk all, and did so, their stature grows, reaching towards tragic heroism. At home, Martha kept faith with them, preserving the letters that brought their story to us, more than one hundred and fifty years later.

Acknowledgments

I am grateful to several people and organizations for their help in writing this book. The members of the General Barton & Stovall History Heritage Association, particularly Mike Griggs, have been generous in providing information about the north Georgia regiments. Cliff Roberts read the entire manuscript. Their well-planned tours and conferences have allowed me to visit many of the battlefields and campsites of Barton's Brigade and to trace its movements in Georgia, Tennessee, Kentucky, and Mississippi. On one such tour, Sid Champion V provided invaluable knowledge of the Battle of Champion Hill. On a separate visit to Vicksburg, Terry Winschel showed me the positions occupied by the Georgia 52nd in Vicksburg and at other relevant locations of the Vicksburg campaign. The archivists in the McArdle Research Library of the Old Courthouse in Vicksburg copied photographs and provided guidance in tracing the Georgia 52nd through their collections. I'm particularly thankful to Elizabeth Joyner, Curator of the Vicksburg National Military Park, who found in her archives a copy of John Douthit's May 6, 1863, letter, which I had never seen. The University of Illinois Library's fine collections have been useful throughout this project. Fellow Douthit descendant Carol Preston has shared family pictures and stories and offered continual encouragement. Jeff Hunter, a descendant of Thomas Farmer Anderson, directed me to information about the Anderson family and has sent copies of documents housed in the Fannin County Courthouse. Hal Jesperson's maps were crucial to my understanding of the Georgia 52nd's positions. My husband, Michael Palencia-Roth, has read the manuscript chapter by chapter and in full, making many valuable suggestions and helping construct the index. Members of the Red Herring Prose Workshop of Champaign-Urbana, Illinois, also critiqued the manuscript and suggested revisions. Finally, I am grateful to the staff at Mercer University Press for their attention to detail while shepherding this volume into print.

Bibliography

BOOKS

Aristotle. *Poetics*. Translated by S. E. Butcher. New York: Hill and Wang, 1966.

Avery, I. W. *The History of the State of Georgia from 1850 to 1881, Embracing Three Important Epochs: The Decade Before the War; The Period of Reconstruction, with Portraits of the Leading Public Men of This Era*. New York: Brown & Derby, 1881.

Ballard, Michael B. *Pemberton: The General Who Lost Vicksburg*. Jackson, MS: University Press of Mississippi, 1999.

Bearss, Edwin Cole. *The Vicksburg Campaign*. Dayton, OH: Morningside Press, vol. 1, 1985; vol. 2, reissue 1991; vol. 3, reissue 1991.

Bierce, Ambrose. *Ambrose Bierce's Civil War*. Edited by William McCann. New York: Wings Books, 1996.

Bonner, James C. *A History of Georgia Agriculture 1732–1860*. Paperback edition. Athens, GA: University of Georgia Press, 2009.

Bothwell, A. J. *The Old Commander: Gen. U.S. Grant, Sketches of His Life in Pen and Pencil*. 1885; reprint, Chicago, IL: Vandercook & Co., 2007.

Calhoun, W. L. *The History of the 42nd Regiment, Georgia Volunteers, Confederate States Army, Infantry*. Atlanta: Sisson Printing, 1900.

Candler, Allen D., editor. *Confederate Records of the State of Georgia*. Vol. 3. Atlanta: C. P. Byrd, State Printer, 1910.

Collins, Richard. *History of Kentucky*. Louisville, KY: John P. Morton & Co., 1924.

Crummer, Wilbur F., *With Grant at Fort Donelson, Shiloh and Vicksburg*. Oak Park, IL: E. C. Crummer & Co., 1915.

Cunningham, H. H. *Doctors in Gray: The Confederate Medical Service*. Baton Rouge: Louisiana State University Press, 1993.

Douthit, Ruth Long, and Davis Douthit. *Here Come the Douthits: Coast to Coast Across Two Centuries*. Columbus, OH: privately published, 1983.

Drake, Rebecca Blackwell, and Bearss, Margie Riddle. *My Dear Wife: Letters to Matilda; The Civil War Letters of Sid and Matilda Champion*. No place, no publisher, third printing, 2006.

Faust, Drew Gilpin. *This Republic of Suffering: Death and the American Civil War*. New York: Vintage Civil War Library, 2009.

Federal Writers' Project. *The WPA Guide to Tennessee*. Knoxville, TN: University of Tennessee Press, 1986. Reprint of 1939 edition published by Viking Press.

Fisher, Noel C. *War at Every Door: Partisan Politics & Guerrilla Violence in East Tennessee 1860–1869*. Chapel Hill: University of North Carolina Press, 1997.

Foote, Shelby. *Fort Sumter to Perryville*. Volume 1 of *The Civil War, A Narrative*. New York: Vintage Books, 1986.

Foster, William Lovelace. *Vicksburg: Southern City Under Siege*. New Orleans: The New Orleans Historic Collection, 1995.

Freemon, Frank R. *Gangrene and Glory: Medical Care During the American Civil War*. Urbana, IL: University of Illinois Press, 2001.

Gaines, W. Craig. *Encyclopedia of Civil War Shipwrecks*. Baton Rouge, LA: LSU Press, 2008.

Goodson, Gary Ray, Sr. *Georgia Confederate 7,000*. "Part I—New Research: Army of Tennessee" (1995); "Part II—Letters and Diaries" (1997); "Part III—The Narrative" (2000). Shawnee, CO: Goodson Enterprises.

Gorsuch, Robert Newton. *Civil War Diaries and Selected Letters of Robert Newton Gorsuch (1839–1913)*. Transcribed by Edith Irene Gorsuch Smith, Horace Greeley Smith, and Everett Gorsuch Smith, Jr. Privately printed, 2012.

Groom, Winston. *Vicksburg*. New York: Alfred A. Knopf, 2009.

Hankinson, Alan. *Vicksburg 1863: Grant Clears the Mississippi*. Campaign Series 26. London: Osprey Publishing Ltd., 1993.

Hardee, William Joseph. *Rifle and Light Infantry Tactics: for the exercise and manoevre of troops when acting as light infantry or riflemen/prepared under the direction of the War Department*. Nashville, TN: J.O. Griffith, 1861.

Harrison, Lowell H. *The Civil War in Kentucky*. Lexington: The University Press of Kentucky, 1975.

Heinl, Robert Debs, Jr. *The Dictionary of Military and Naval Quotations*. Annapolis, MD: Naval Institute Press, 1966.

Henderson, Lillian. *Roster of the Confederate Soldiers of Georgia, 1861–1865*. Volume 5. Hapeville, GA: Longino & Porter, Inc., 1960.

Humes, Thomas William. *The Loyal Mountaineers of Tennessee*. Knoxville, TN: Ogden Bros. & Co., 1888.

Jones, Ethelene Dyer, and Dale Dyer, editors. *Facets of Fannin: A History of Fannin County, Georgia.* Dallas, TX: Curtis Media Corporation, 1989.

Kountz, John S. *Record of the Organizations Engaged in the Campaign, Siege and Defense of Vicksburg.* Washington, D.C.: Government Printing Office, 1901.

Krakow, Ken K. *Georgia Place-Names.* 3rd edition. Macon, GA: Winship Press, 1999. Online edition at http://www.kenkrakow.com/gpn/georgia_place-names.htm.

Lane, Mills, editor. *"Dear Mother: Don't grieve about me. If I get killed, I'll only be dead": Letters from Georgia Soldiers in the Civil War.* Savannah, GA: The Beehive Press, 1990.

Lanman, Charles. *Letters from the Alleghany Mountains.* New York: George P. Putnam, 1849.

McPherson, James. *Battle Cry of Freedom: The Civil War Era.* New York: Oxford University Press, 1988.

Matthews, James M., editor. *The Statutes at Large of the Provisional Government of the Confederate States of America from the Institution of the Government February 8, 1861, to its Termination, February 18, 1862, Inclusive.* Richmond, VA: R.M. Smith, 1864.

Mooney, James. *Myths of the Cherokee and Sacred Formulas of the Cherokees.* Nashville, TN: Charles and Randy Elder Booksellers, 1982.

Moore, Albert Burton. *Conscription and Conflict in the Confederacy.* New York: Macmillan Co., 1924.

Moore, Frank, editor. *Rebellion Record: A Diary of American Events.* Volume 4. New York: Van Nostrand, 1865.

Moose, Virge [Frederick V.], *War Reminsces: A Collection of War Stories as Remembered by Virge Moose, Company C, 52nd Georgia Infantry Regiment, Army of Tennessee—Confederate States of America, as they appeared in the* Dahlonega Signal, *1981.* Compiled with preface by Cynthia Adair Coan, undated photocopy in softcover.

Pittenger, William. *Daring and Suffering: A History of the Andrews Raid into Georgia in 1862.* New York: The War Publishing Company, 1887.

Rozema, Vicki. *Footsteps of the Cherokee: A Guide to the Eastern Homelands of the Cherokee Nation.* Winston-Salem, NC: John F. Blair Publisher, 2000.

Sarris, Jonathan Dean. *A Separate Civil War: Communities in Conflict in the Mountain South.* Charlottesville, VA: University of Virginia Press, 2006.

Scaife, William R., and William Harris Bragg. *Joe Brown's Pets: The Georgia Militia 1861–1865*. Macon, GA: Mercer University Press, 2004.

Sears, Stephen W., editor. The Civil War. 3 volumes. Vol. 1: *The First Year Told by Those Who Lived It*; vol. 2: *The Second Year Told by Those Who Lived It*; vol. 3: *The Third Year Told by Those Who Lived It*. New York: The Library of America, 2011, 2012, 2013.

Shea, William L., and Terrence J. Winschel. *Vicksburg Is the Key: The Struggle for the Mississippi River*. Lincoln, NE: University of Nebraska Press, 2003.

Sherman, William Tecumseh. Edited by Charles Royster. *Memoirs of General W. T. Sherman*. New York: Library of America, 1990.

Simon, F. Kevin, editor. *The WPA Guide to Kentucky*. Lexington, KY: University Press of Kentucky, 1996. Reprint of 1939 edition published by Harcourt Brace.

Smith, Timothy B. *Champion Hill: Decisive Battle for Vicksburg*. New York: Savas Beatie, Civil War Preservation Trust Special Edition, 2007.

Thompson, Kathy, editor. *Touching Home: A Collection of History and Folklore from the Copper Basin, Fannin County Area*. Orlando, FL: Daniels Publishers, 1976.

Twain, Mark. *Life on the Mississippi*. Edited by James M. Cox. New York: Penguin Books, 1984.

Walker, Peter F. *Vicksburg: A People at War, 1860–1865*. Chapel Hill, NC: University of North Carolina Press, 1960.

Watkins, Sam R. *Co. Aytch: A Confederate Memoir of the Civil War*. 1882; reprint, New York: Simon & Schuster, 2003.

Williams, David, Teresa Crisp Williams, and David Carlson. *Plain Folk in a Rich Man's War: Class and Dissent in Confederate Georgia*. Gainesville: University Press of Florida, 2002.

DOCUMENTS

Civil War Service Records, National Archives.

Denson, J. "The Phrenological character of John M. Douthit as inferred by Prof. J. Denson July 24, 1858." Copy of handwritten document, owned by author.

Deposition of Thomas Anderson, February 8, 1877; and Report of Special Agent John G. Wager, March 8, 1877. Pension Case file of Solomon Stansbury RG 15, National Archives.

Fannin County, Georgia, Court Papers, volume titled "Miscellaneous, 1858--."

Fannin County, Georgia Deed Book D.

Fannin County, Georgia, District 1029, Handwritten Civil War muster rolls.

US Federal Census Reports for Fannin County, Georgia. 1860, 1870, 1880.

US War Department. *The War of the Rebellion: A Compilation of the Official Records of the Union and Confederate Armies.* 128 volumes. Washington, D.C.: Government Printing Office, 1880–1901.

ARTICLES

Adams, George Worthington. "Confederate Medicine." *Journal of Southern History* 6/2 (May 1940): 151–66.

———. "Caring for the Men." National Historical Society. *The Image of War 1861–1865*, volume 4. Garden City, NY: Doubleday & Co., 1983. 231–74.

Austin, Francis. "Letter Writing in a Cornish Community in the 1790s." In *Letter Writing as a Social Practice*, edited by David Barton and Nigel Hall. Philadelphia: John Benjamins Publ., 2000. 43–61.

Camp, Raleigh S. "'What I Know I Know, and I Dare Express It': Major Raleigh S. Camp's History of the Georgia 40th Infantry in the Vicksburg Campaign." *Civil War Regiments* 5/1 (1996–1997): 45–91.

Curtis, Henry Clay. "Story of the Thomas Wilson Family." *Fannin County Times.* Series of articles, April–July 1956. Also, photocopied typescript of same material.

Davis, Robert S., Jr. With assistance from Bill Kinsland. "Forgotten Union Guerillas of the North Georgia Mountains." *North Georgia Journal* 5/2 (summer 1988): 30–49.

———. "White and Black in Blue: The Recruitment of Federal Units in Civil War North Georgia." *Georgia Historical Quarterly* 85/3 (fall 2001): 347–74.

Ford, Emily. Blog of Oak and Laurel Cemetery Preservation LLC. New Orleans. www.oakandlaurel.com.

Fowler, Nolan. "Johnny Reb's Impressions of Kentucky in the Fall of 1862." *The Register of the Kentucky Historical Society* 48/164 (July 1950): 205–15.

General Barton & Stovall History Heritage Association. *GBSHHA Newsletter.* Electronic edition, 2013–2018.

Hewitt, Lawrence Lee. "Braxton Bragg Reconsidered." *Civil War Times* 53/1 (February 2014): 30–37.

Kelley, Mitchell. "The Campbell Salt Springs Guards: A History of Company K, 41st Regiment, Georgia Volunteer Infantry, Army of Ten-

nessee, CSA." Published on
http://www.rootsweb.ancestry.com/~gacampbe/Company_K_History
.htm.

Kinsland, William S. "The 52nd Regiment, Georgia Infantry." *North Geor-gia Journal* 2/2 (summer 1985): 8–30.

Lee, Stephen Dill. "The Campaign of Vicksburg, Mississippi, in 1863—From April 15 to and including The Battle of Champion Hills, or Bakers Creek, May 16, 1863." *Publications of the Mississippi Historical Society* 3 (1900): 21–53.

"Mail Service and the Civil War," unauthored, at
https://about.usps.com/news/national-releases/2012/pr12_civil-war-mail-history.pdf.

Parks, William Asbury. "Sketches and Incidents in the Confederate Ar-my." *Wesleyan Christian Advocate*, March 8, 1899.

Provine, William B. "The Legend of 'Long Tom' at Cumberland Gap." *Tennessee Historical Quarterly* 24/3 (fall 1965): 256–64.

Ranck, Ethan. "Cypress Grove II Cemetery."
https://neworleanshistorical.org/items/show/1253.

Stevenson, B. F. "Cumberland Gap, a paper read before the Ohio com-mandery of the military order of the Loyal Legion of the United States, June 3, 1885, by companion B. F. Stevenson, late Surgeon (Major) 22nd Kentucky Volunteer Infantry." Cincinnati: H.C. Sherick & Co., 1885. Pamphlet.

NEWSPAPERS

The Confederate Union (Milledgeville, GA) 24/27 (November 24, 1863).
Fannin County Times (Blue Ridge, GA) 26 (1956).
Memphis Daily Appeal (Atlanta, GA) 14/269 (December 24, 1863).
Southern Banner (Athens, GA) 31/47 (January 28, 1863).
Southern Confederacy (Atlanta, GA) 2/20 (March 8, 1862); 2/88 (May 29, 1862); 2/20 (April 15, 1862).
Southern Federal Union (Milledgeville, GA) 33/12 (August 12, 1862).
Southern Recorder (Milledgeville, GA) 43/9 (March 4, 1862).
Southern Watchman (Athens, GA) 8/5 (May 1, 1861).

LETTERS

Campbell, Capt. W. A. to Henry C. Wayne, A.G., April 24, 1861. Con-federate Service Records, National Archives.

Crumley, Leander F., to wife Nancy E. Crumley, 1862–1863. Originals and transcripts published by the Crumley family on the website files.usgarchives.net/ga/Madison/history/letters/ crumley.

Douthit, John M., to Martha Willson Douthit and Juliette Condecy Douthit, March 20, 1862–May 6, 1863. Privately owned.

Goodman, John, to John Mitchell Davidson, May 28, 1862. Letters of the Davidson family, Davidson family papers, Transcripts, box 2, folder 3 (January–June 1862). Housed at the Atlanta History Center and available online at www.dlg.galileo.usg.edu.

Murphy, Matthias, to his brother-in-law, Redding Floyd, January 18, 1863. Photocopy and transcript, McCardle Research Library, Old Courthouse, Vicksburg, MS.

Robinson, Henry W., collection of 38 letters, Stuart A. Rose Manuscript, Archives, and Rare Book Library, Emory University.

Willson, John Vandiver, to US Adjutant General, October 10, 1864. National Archives.

Index

Douthit, Davis (John M.'s brother), see Douthit, Warren Davis

Douthit, Harriet Garren, 4, 14, 56, 118, 119, 123, 155, 165

Douthit, Harriet Magness, 4

Douthit, John (1709-1784), 9

Douthit, John (1798-1851), 3, 4

Douthit, John (cousin of John M. Douthit), 32, 66, 79

Douthit, John M., xi, xii, xiii, xiv, xv, 2, 3, 4, 9, 11, 12, 14, 15, 17, 20, 23, 25, 26, 29, 30, 32, 33, 40, 41, 47, 49, 51, 52, 57, 66, 79, 82, 93, 96, 100, 103, 106, 107, 111, 127, 128, 141, 146, 147, 148, 149, 150, 151, 153, 154, 155, 156, 157, 159, 160, 161, 164, 166, 167, 169, 171, 172, 173

Letters: March 2, 1862, 18-19; June 7, 1862, 31; June 16, 1862, 36-37; June 24, 1862, 42-43; June 28, 1862, 43-44; July 3, 1862, 45-46; July 17, 1862, 49-50; July 26, 1862, 54-55; July 27, 1862, 55-56; n.d. (summer 1862), 58; August 21, 1862, 59; September 7, 1862, 61-63; September 10, 1862, 63-64; September 18, 1862, 65; October 28, 1862, 67-77; November 11, 1862, 84-85; November 12, 1862, 85-86; November 27, 1862, 87-88; December 4, 1862, 90-91; December 12, 1862, 91-92; January 1, 1863, 101-02; February 2, 1863, 112-13; February 8, 1863, 114-15; March 1, 1863, 116; March 19, 1863, 117; April 7, 1863, 118-19; April 16, 1863, 119-20; April 30, 1863, 121; May 2, 1863, 122-23; May 6, 1863, 124-25

Douthit, Julietta ("Julitty"), see Curtis, Julietta "Julitty" Douthit

Douthit, Lilly Ann McClure, 3, 5, 118

Douthit, Lorenzo Maxfield, 164

Douthit, Martha Emeline Willson, see Anderson, Martha Emeline Willson Douthit

Douthit, Nannie, 156

Douthit, Rebecka, see Weaver, Rebeckah Douthit

Douthit, Robert (John M.'s brother) 3-4

Douthit, Robert (John M.'s uncle), 32

Douthit, Silas, 66, 79

Douthit, Solomon (John M.'s grandfather), 12

Douthit, Solomon M. (John M.'s brother), 3, 9, 11, 14, 49, 52, 55, 102, 117, 165

Douthit, Victoria Jane, see Cochran, Victoria Jane Douthit

Douthit, Warren Davis, xii, 4, 9, 11, 14, 55, 56, 117, 118, 119, 123, 127, 128, 138, 146, 147, 148, 149, 150, 151, 153, 154, 155, 156, 157, 159, 165, 166, 171, 172, 173

Edom, GA, 4

Edwards Station (Depot), MS, 127, 128, 129, 131, 133, 139

El Dorado, KY, 70, 73

Ellet, Charles, Jr., 113

Ellet, Charles Rivers, Col., 113

Ellijay, GA, 32

Emancipation Proclamation, 102

Etowah River, 18

Fall, Philip, 97

Fannin, James Walker, Jr., Col., 10

Fannin County, GA, xi, 1, 2, 3, 4, 5, 6, 7, 9, 10, 14, 17, 20, 52, 53, 86, 115, 117, 145, 147, 156, 158, 159, 160, 161, 162, 164, 165, 166

Farragut, David, Adm., 139

Faust, Drew Gilpin, 156, 157

190